VOL.5

JOURNAL OF ARMORED

ASSAULT

&

HELIBORNE WARFARE

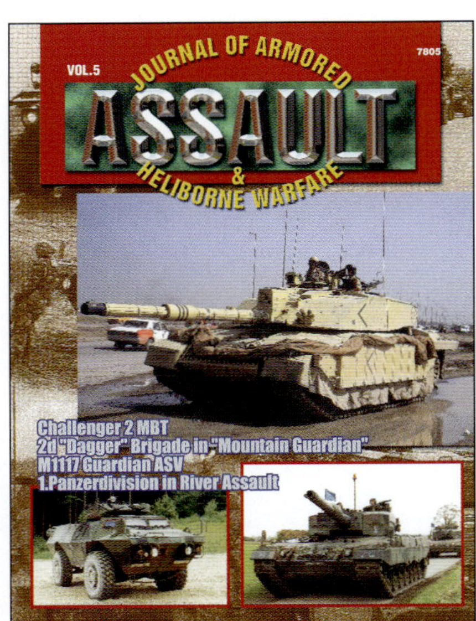

Editor: James R. Hill
Copyright © 2003
by CONCORD PUBLICATIONS CO.
603-609 Castle Peak Road
Kong Nam Industrial Building
10/F, B1, Tsuen Wan
New Territories, Hong Kong
www.concord-publications.com

We welcome authors who can help expand our range of books. If you would like to submit material, please feel free to contact us.

We are always on the look-out for new, unpublished photos for this series. If you have photos or slides or information you feel may be useful to future volumes, please send them to us for possible future publication. Full photo credits will be given upon publication.

ISBN 962-361-071-8
printed in Hong Kong

Union Jack Armor Might
Britain's Challenger 2 MBT <u>Carl Schulze</u>

Belonging to B Squadron Queen´s Royal Lancers these two Challenger 2 were seen in the outskirts of Basra. The picture was taken shortly after Challenger 2 stopped an attack of 14 Iraqi T-55. Well visible on the vehicles is the IFF (Identification Friend Foe) System adopted by the British forces during the war. The system uses panels with metal plates which have a different heat signature from the rest of the vehicle. When seen through a thermal imaging sight like the TOGS II of Challenger 2 the panel provides a square black dot in the picture. (Courtesy: UK MoD)

The 2003 Gulf War (Operation "Iraqi Freedom") was the true baptism of fire for the British Army's Challenger 2 Main Battle Tank (MBT) in actual combat operations. 120 Challenger 2 of the Germany-based 7th Armoured Brigade, the legendary "Desert Rats," deployed to Kuwait in early February 2003. When war broke out on March 20, 2003 the Challenger 2 of the Royal Scots Dragoon Guards and the 2nd Royal Tank Regiment, reinforced by vehicles from the Queen's Royal Lancers, were among the first British vehicles to enter Iraq. In the weeks to follow Challenger 2-equipped units saw extensive combat, one such engagement took place during the night of March 26-27 when A Squadron, The Royal Scots Dragoon Guards eliminated an Iraqi tank unit and infantry positions near Basra. During the war, it should be noted, not a single Challenger 2 was lost to enemy fire, while there were at least six U.S. M1A1 Abrams destroyed in action. In fact, the only Challenger 2 lost during the war belonged to the Queen's Royal Lancers and it was hit by friendly fire—during the extensive fighting near Basra on March 25, this Challenger was engaged and damaged by another tank in the unit; in this incident two of the four crew-members were killed and the others injured. The story of Britain's Challenger 2, is one of technology, tradition and now, combat-proven mettle.

History and Development

The Challenger 2 MBT was developed and built by Vickers Defence Systems, a company that has more than eighty-years of tradition in developing and producing tanks, including the first tanks ever used in battle. Since 2002 Vickers Defence Systems is part of Alvis Plc. The Challenger 2 program started in 1986 as a private venture of Vickers Defence. The company believed that the British Army would soon need a replacement for its fleet of Chieftain MBTs. 420 previously-purchased Challenger 1 MBTs had only replaced approximately half of the ageing and minimally (by 1990-standards) armored Chieftain MBT fleet. The company also saw other potential markets for MBTs—primarily in the Middle East. The fact that Vickers Defence Systems purchased the vehicle business branch of Royal Ordnance Factory in the same year benefited the program. This allowed Vickers to combine its development of the Vickers Mk 7 MBT with the lessons learned during development of the Challenger 1 by Royal Ordnance. Development of the Challenger 2 was based on the in-service Challenger 1 MBT implementing Mk 7 MBT technology. First proposals including a program demonstration were made to the British Ministry of Defence (MoD) in 1987. In 1988 the MoD issued a staff requirement and Vickers Defence Systems submitted a formal proposal. During the same year the first of nine prototype turrets was built. The MoD placed a proof of principle contract as a first stage in its competitive procurement program for "Chieftain Replacement" in 1989. In September 1990, with already nine prototypes existing, the proof of principle phase finished. Of the nine prototypes seven were built at the Vickers Defence Systems facility in Leeds, while the remaining two were manufactured at the company's facility in Newcastle-upon-Tyne. All prototypes of Challenger 2 differed in minor ways and only the last one –Prototype 9—incorporated all 156 hull improvements made to the original Challenger 1 chassis. During the development of the Challenger 2 the prototypes clocked up 20,400 km of road and cross-country driving and fired 11,600 rounds of 120mm ammunition. After an international competition involving Challenger 2 (UK), Abrams M1A2 (USA), Leopard 2A5 (Germany) and Leclerc (France), the MoD placed a first order for 127 Challenger 2 MBTs and thirteen driver training tanks in June 1991. The first training tanks were delivered in 1993 well in advance to the MBTs, of which the first left the factory in July 1994. In 1994 the British Army formally accepted the Challenger 2; an additional order for 259 MBT and 9 more driver training tanks soon followed. This order became necessary

On June 30, 1998, the first Challenger 2 was formally handed over to the British Army. Part of the ceremony was a live firing demonstration involving the five tanks which can be seen lined up here. The ceremony took place on "Range No. 9" at the Bergen Hohne training area in Germany. During the demonstration the tanks fired from a static position onto static targets at a range between 1,500 and 2,800 meters using the "Hunter and Killer" mode. In addition the tank's capability to fire at and hit a moving target while moving itself was demonstrated. The demonstration was conducted by the Royal Scots Dragoon Guards to whom the pictured tanks belong.

when the MoD decided to replace the Challenger 1 in service due to reliability and performance issues. Another reason for the order was the defense cuts following the break down of the former Warsaw Pact, culminating in the restructuring of British tank forces and their drastic reduction in numbers of tanks, calling for a more capable weapon system.

After the initially produced Challenger 2 MBTs were delivered to the Royal Armoured School in Bovington, the first unit to receive Britain's new MBT was the Royal Scots Dragoon Guards based in Germany; they received their first Challenger 2s in March 1998. On June 30, 1998, Sir Collin Chandler, Chairman of Vickers Plc, formally handed over the first of 386 Challenger 2 to the British Army, represented by Major-General J. P. Kiszely MC, CO 1 (UK) Armoured Division, Lieutenant-Colonel A.M. Phillips, CO The Royal Scots Dragoon Guards, Lieutenant-General Sir Robert Hayman-Joyce KCB, CBE, DL, Deputy Chief Of Defence Procurement (Operations) and Master General Of The Ordnance, and General Jack Deverell, Deputy Commander-in-Chief British Land Forces. The ceremony took place on Range 9 at the Bergen Hohne training area in Germany. The ceremony was combined with a tank platoon live fire power demonstration to demonstrate the capabilities of the new tanks. This demonstration started with a small description of the tank, followed by a tank firing from a static position onto static targets at a range between 1,500 and 2,800 meters using the "Hunter and Killer" mode. All eight targets were destroyed within forty-seconds. This demonstration was followed by an attack of three Challenger 2 firing at various targets including bunkers and enemy tanks using the vehicle's ability to fire at and hit a moving target while moving itself. In 1999 the Challenger 2 passed the In-Service-Reliability-Demonstration (ISRD). During the ISRD a squadron of twelve Challenger 2 MBTs was put through a series of demanding trials under battlefield conditions by the Armoured Trials and Development Unit (ATDU) at the Royal Armoured Corps Centre at Bovington, Dorset. Manned by British Army crews the tanks run through eighty-four simulated battlefield days. During each of these days each tank covered thirty-three kilometers cross country and twenty-seven kilometers on the road, fired thirty-four rounds with its 120mm main gun and 1,000 rounds with its 7.62mm coaxial chain gun. After this impressive and all-important rite of passage, the ISRD Vickers Defence Systems could proudly state that Challenger 2 had outperformed the reliability targets set by the MoD.

In January 2000 the Royal Scots Dragoon Guards was the first unit to deploy on an operation with Challenger 2 when the regiment formed part of Operation "Agricola 3," as Britain's commitment to the multinational peacekeeping operation in Kosovo was called. Sixteen Challenger 2 MBTs were deployed under the Multinational Brigade Central of KFOR and was deployed to deter the Yugoslav Army from entering into Kosovo and extremists from conducting violent actions against other ethnic groups. Since this first deployment, Challenger 2 MBTs have regularly seen operational service with the peace support missions of KFOR in Kosovo and SFOR in Bosnia.

During the official handover ceremony held in Germany on June 30, 1998, this Challenger 2 of the Royal Scots Dragoon Guards is fitted with a special exhaust system which was also used during the 2003 Gulf War. In addition the vehicle is equipped with a new type of camouflage netting which reduces the radar and heat signature of the tank.

The business end of a Royal Scots Dragoon Guards Challenger 2 main armament cannon. The vehicle belongs to the first vehicles handed over to the regiment and was involved in the official handover ceremony held in Germany on June 30, 1998. The Challenger 2 has a crew of four consisting of commander, gunner driver and loader. In the picture the commander and loader can be seen in the open hatches of the turret. The driver is situated in front of the turret in the middle of the chassis and the gunner is seated in the turret just in front of the commander on the right side.

Today, the Challenger 2 is the only MBT in service with the British Army, carrying the fighting vehicle number FV 218100 given by the Ministry of Defence. The last of the 386 Challenger 2 MBTs were handed over to the British Army during a ceremony on the April 17, 2002. This last vehicle was built at the Newcastle-upon-Tyne facility of Vickers Defence. The Leeds facility produced Challenger 2 up to 1999, when work was completed. In addition to the Challenger 2 MBTs, the project included the development, production and delivery of the CHARM 3 ammunition system and a full support package including training equipment and initial spares. Currently the only export customer for Challenger 2 is the Sultanate of Oman; the country placed its first order for Challenger 2 MBTs in 1993. This order was for eighteen Challenger 2 MBTs and two driver training tanks. The first Omani Challenger 2 was delivered in 1995. Another twenty Challenger 2 MBTs were ordered by Oman in 1997 and delivered in 2000. In the Royal Omani Army Challenger 2 is used by the 1st Tank Regiment, based at Shaffa.

A Tour of the Challenger 2 Chassis

The hull and chassis of Challenger 2 is "virtually" identical to that of that of the Challenger 1, but a closer look reveals 156 improvements. These include a new track made by Blair Catton with a double pin design and a track width of 650mm, having a service live of 5,000 kilometers. An improved track will enter service in 2003, this will increase track service live to approximately 8,000 kilometers. To change the MBT's track takes

This Challenger 2 of the Royal Scots Dragoon Guards is fitted with the Live Firing Monitoring Equipment (LFME) which can be seen on the right rear of the turret. With the LFME system, live fire is monitored by gunnery instructors of the Royal Armored Corps. The equipment allows the instructors to explain mistakes easier to the tank soldiers by using recorded intercom sequences between the tank crew or between the tanks of a platoon and by video sequences that are filmed through the sights of each tank showing what the commander and gunner have seen from "their" vantage point. The system works with a microwave TV link between each tank and the control container, where the instructors get the information in real time and where the data is recorded. The LFME is made by Wegmann, a German-firm.

Together with Challenger 2 an impressive range of training aids from wall pictures to highly sophisticated simulators was issued to the regiments. Initially used for conversion training, today the training equipment is used to keep the crews on a high training level while at the same time—most importantly in these frugal days—cutting costs. Here the turret gunnery trainer room of the Queens Royal Lancers based in Osnabrück, Germany can be seen to advantage. Three trainers can be linked together and allow to train complex battle situations on troop level.

During their conversion training from Challenger 1 to Challenger 2 troops from the Queens Royal Lancers can be seen using manuals while getting introduced to the turret systems. In addition to the manuals a computer program was issued to the Challenger 2 units focused on teaching technical data and theoretical knowledge by the use of multiple choice tests in several levels. Each soldier has his personal password and can only proceed to a higher level if he has passed the previous test. This use of computer technology allow each soldier to learn about the Challenger 2 tank in his own speed and makes sure that he had the required knowledge before entering the next level.

the crew between twelve and twenty-four hours, but in the near future this number will be reduced by the introduction of the "Complete Track Delivery System" also known as CTDS. With CTDS the tracks for a tank will be delivered in two parts for each side and track mounting time will be reduced drastically. The hydraulic track tensioner at the vehicle front can be used by the driver to tension the track correctly from under armor. The hypo pneumatic suspension of Challenger 2 is basically the same system as in the Challenger 1, but new seals have been fitted and the complete system is upgraded. Challenger 2 uses the same power pack that was fitted to Challenger 1, the Perkins 12-cylinder twin turbocharged diesel CV-12 TCA Condor V-12, which is coupled to the David Brown TN54 vehicle transmission with six forward, and two reverse, gears. In total this provides the Challenger 2, which has got a combat weight of 64 tons, with a maximum road speed of 59 km/hr on roads, and 40 km/hr when moving cross-country at high speed. For easier steering the driver's controls are more rugged. With its fuel capacity of 1,592-liters the tank has a road range of 450-kilometers; if the two fire retardant 175-liter drum type fuel tanks at the rear are used to store additional fuel the road ranged is increased by an additional 100-kilometers. The internal fuel tanks have been changed to fire retardant bag type ones. The engine compartment and engine decks are redesigned to allow easier access during maintenance and repair duties. When asked, British soldiers gave a time of three-to-four hours for changing the whole power pack. Inside the engine bay a Graviner fire suppression system is fitted and the engine construction allows the

This photograph shows a Challenger 2 commander ready in his position in the turret. The picture was taken in the turret gunnery trainer and gives a good impression of the conditions inside the turret. The commander is looking in the eyepiece of the fully SFIM stabilized panoramic sight VS 580-10. The sight is mounted on the turret roof and has a magnification of x3.2 and x10.5 by day and also contains an Nd-YAG laser range finder.

Inside the gun trainer the loader is trained. In addition of loading the gun with various types of ammunition, training sessions include the loading of the chain gun and the dealing with mail functions. Mail functions might include the jamming of the coaxial machine gun, miss fires of the 120mm gun or even mechanical failures on the gun system. The picture is taken from the top rear left of the turret showing the loader's place.

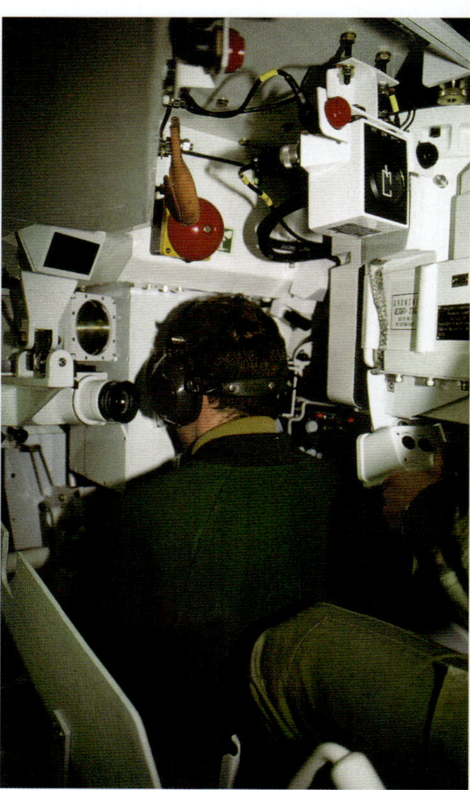

Even in the latest MBTs, like the Challenger 2, the gunner's position is always crammed. The controls for the TOGS II and the Gunner's Primary Sight combine a 4Hz laser range finder with a x3 and x10 magnification.

Challenger 2 of A Squadron the Royal Scots Dragoon Guards on the Bergen Hohne ranges. On the turret of the tank a number of practice HESH rounds called PRAC SH L32A6 are stored. Soon the crew will handle them and store them properly inside the turret. Challenger 2 uses ammunition which consists of a separate round, primer and charge.

During conversion training of the Queens Royal Lancers from Challenger 1 to Challenger 2, an officer can be seen acting as loader in the gun trainer. He is just loading a HESH round. Well visible is the split block sliding breech mechanism with elastomeric obturating pad of the main gun system of Challenger 2.

The crew conversion from Challenger 1 to Challenger 2 took six weeks of gunnery training including day and night live firing exercises. During this period each gunner fires approximately forty rounds. The training included firing on standing or moving targets at different distances while the tank stands or moves. All of this was watched by gunnery instructors of the Royal Armoured Corps using the Live Firing Monitoring Equipment (LFME) which is made by Wegmann in Germany and can be seen here mounted on the turret rear. Next to it a couple of HESH rounds and machine gun ammunition for the next phase of live firing training can be seen.

injection of diesel fuel into the exhaust outlets (left and right) to generate a smoke screen which hides the vehicle if necessary. The layout of the chassis is conventional with the driver seated at the front, the turret being mounted in the center and the engine bay being situated to the rear. The driver enters and leaves his compartment via a single piece hatch which swings forward horizontally. For night driving the driver is equipped with an image intensifying Passive Driving Periscope. The periscope uses a night vision image intensifier device which allows the tank to achieve speeds comparable to day-time speeds. The running gear of Challenger 2 consists of six road wheels, a rear drive sprocket, a front idler and two track return rollers on either side.

The Challenger 2 Turret

The key technological breakthrough that makes the Challenger 2 such a lethal MBT is its highly sophisticated yet easy to use weapon system. This allows the crew to acquire, identify and achieve an accurate laser range to a target at a range of up to 9-kilometers and once the target is in range of the 55 caliber 120mm L30 rifled tank gun it can be destroyed, no matter if either Challenger 2 or the target or both are moving or standing still. This is possible due to the all-electric gun control and stabilization system which incorporates a MIL-STD-1553 data bus and stabilizes the gun system as well as the gunner's and commander's sights vertically and horizontally. The fire control computer of the tank can engage two targets at the same time, this in fact means that after a target is identified and the tank commander has laid the dot in the center of his roof-mounted sight on the target he switches it over to the gunner together with the fire order including ammunition type as well as type of target. The computer then sets the gun and automatically lays the gunner's sight on the target and the engagement is continued by the gunner. The tank commander's sight, which can traverse 360° totally independent from the turret, is free and he can use it to engage the next target. If he discovers a target with greater priority he can use the commander's fire control override to destroy this target first by either switching it to the gunner or using his own controls to place the aiming marks on the target, fire the laser for range-finding and then press the fire button for the 120mm gun. If he does not use this system the commander presses his align switch to move the gun onto the already laser-pinpointed target after the gunner has destroyed target number one. Now the computer immediately traverses the turret to target number two, lays the gun and fires it automatically. To reach a high grade of accuracy the tank is fitted with a meteorological sensor which provides all weather details important for firing to the computer, including wind direction and strength, air pressure and temperature, humidity and other climactic conditions and factors. The commander's fully SFIM stabilized panoramic sight VS 580-10 is mounted on the turret roof and has a magnification of x3.2 and x10.5 by day and also contains an Nd-YAG laser rangefinder. The sight provides all round vision without the commander having to move his head. The elevation range is plus or minus thirty-five degrees. In addition to this a Thermal Observation and Gunnery Sight II (TOGS II) thermal imaging system x4 or x11.5 can be used by feeding its picture into the sight. The gunner's stabilized Gunner's Primary Sight combines the same model of 4Hz laser range finder with a x3 and x10 magnification and is also mounted on the turret roof, it has a traverse of 7° left and right. The laser rangefinder with a wavelength of 1.064 microns can be used on a range between 200 meters and ten kilometers while the range accuracy is +/- 5 meters. The gunner is also equipped with a reversionary mode L30 telescope mounted coaxially with the main gun. The sights of Challenger 2 are protected by armored hoods/cowls. Both commander and driver have a monitor to the left of their sights providing the TOGS II picture for relaxed observation in surveillance situations. The TOGS II is mounted above the gun with which it moves coaxially. Gunner and commander are placed on the right turret side, to the right of the tank gun, behind each other with the commander positioned slightly higher.

The 120mm L30 rifled tank gun of the Challenger 2 can fire most current British 120mm rounds including APFSDS-T, HESH and Smoke projectiles. In addition the newly developed L27A1 APFSDS Depleted Uranium (DU) round of the CHARM 3 system using the new L17A1 stick charge propellant system can be fired. The Challenger 2 uses ammunition which consists of a separate round and charge. Here practice HESH rounds called PRAC SH L32A6 can be seen stored on the turret prior to the moment when they will be placed in the armored bins inside.

The crew of a Challenger 2 loads their tank with the meat and potatoes of their profession—the rounds for the 120mm L30 rifled tank gun. While the last charge is given to the loader inside the turret, where it will be stored below the turret ring, on the turret practice rounds DS PRAC L20A1 can be seen.

After the charges have been stored in the storage bins under the turret ring the rounds are handed down into the turret in order to be stored in the armored bins of the turret.

The muzzle of the 120mm 55 caliber L30 rifled tank gun of a Challenger 2 of the Royal Scots Dragoon Guards.

Close-up photograph of the armor protected housing of TOGS II thermal imaging sight of Challenger 2.

The loader sits on the left side of the turret, at the same side of the main gun the 7.62mm coaxial L94A1 Chain Gun, designed by McDonnell Douglas, is mounted. The L94A1 Chain Gun is also used in the British Army Warrior infantry fighting vehicle. The loader has a 7.62mm GPMG anti-air machine gun, type L37A2, mounted on the cupola. Both the commander and the loader have a single-piece hatch cover that opens to the rear. For observation purposes the loader has a single roof-mounted day periscope that can be traversed. The turret is capable of 360 degree rotation and the 120mm L30 rifled tank gun has an elevation range from -10 to +20 degrees. On each side at the front of the turret a bank of five L8 smoke grenade dischargers is mounted. As mentioned above, Challenger 2 can also set a smoke screen by injecting diesel fuel into the engine exhausts. The armor of the Challenger 2 turret is the latest version of Chobham armor—known as "Dorchester Armour." This armor increases the battlefield survivability of Challenger 2 against attacks with kinetic energy ammunition as well as against attacks with chemical energy ammunition. The totally new designed turret, together with the rest of the hull, also incorporates stealth technology to minimize the radar signature of the vehicle. To protect the vehicle against NBC threats Challenger 2 is equipped with a fighting compartment over-pressure system that filters the air and also provides climate control. This system is mounted in the rear of the turret bustle.

Gun and Ammunition

The 55 caliber 120mm L30 rifled tank gun of the Challenger 2 can fire most *current* British 120mm rounds including APFSDS-T, HESH and Smoke projectiles. In addition the newly developed L27A1 APFSDS Depleted Uranium (DU) round of the CHARM 3 system using the new L17A1 stick charge propellant system can be fired, as well. Depleted Uranium has a density approximately two-and-a-half times higher than that of steel and the mass of the DU projectile provides high penetration characteristics. Similar to Challenger 1, the Challenger 2 uses ammunition which consists of a separate round and charge. The ammunition is stored with its explosive components under the turret ring while the charges are stored above in armored bins. Depending on the role of a Challenger 2 within its regiment, and the number of radios fitted in the turret, the numbers of rounds carried by the tank can vary from forty-three to forty-nine rounds. In addition to the ammunition of the main armament inside the tank 4,200 rounds of 7.62mm ammunition are available for the two machine guns. The L30 gun barrel is made of ESR (electro-slag refined) steel, auto-frettaged, chrome-lined and fitted with a thermal sleeve, fume extractor and muzzle reference system. The chrome-lining of the barrel gives it a longer live and more consistent accuracy. In addition it allows an increased velocity and therefore gives the round more penetration power. A fume extraction system is fitted to the gun to remove gasses from the barrel and prevent them from entering the fighting compartment. The gun has a split-block sliding breech mechanism with an elastomeric obturating pad.

Challenger 2E

Designed for the export market, the Challenger 2E is the latest version of Challenger 2 and was designed to cope with harsh environmental and climatic conditions. The modifications carried out on Challenger 2E include the fitting of a new power pack—known as the Europack—that includes a transversely mounted MTU 883 diesel engine coupled to a Renk HSWL 295TM automatic transmission. The Renk transmission features five forward and three reverse gears. The engine,

This Challenger 2 belongs to the Royal Scots Dragoon Guards and is crossing a water obstacle on Drawsko Pomorski Training Area on a ferry made by M3 amphibious rigs in 1999. The diagram and number code on the turret side identify the vehicle as the tank of the squadron commander of B Squadron. 0B stands for officer commanding and the rectangle identifies the squadron. A Squadron is marked with a triangle, C Squadron is marked with a circle, D Squadron uses a rectangle and HQ Squadron uses a diamond. Other codes used with the diagrams on the MBTs of an armored regiment are as follow:

-11B	*CO (Commanding Officer of the regiment)*
-22B	*II IC (Second in Command of the regiment)*
-0B	*OC (Officer Commanding a squadron)*
-0C	*Squadron II IC (Second in Command of a squadron)*
-10	*Troop Commander 1st Troop*
-20	*Troop Commander 2nd Troop*
-30	*Troop Commander 3rd Troop*
-40	*Troop Commander 4th Troop*
-11 and 12	*Gun tanks of 1st Troop*
-21 and 22	*Gun tanks of 2nd Troop*
-31 and 32	*Gun tanks of 3rd Troop*
-41 and 42	*Gun tanks of 4th Troop*

Two Challenger 2 MBTs from the Royal Scots Dragoon Guards are ferried over one of the countless water obstacles on Drawsko Pomorski Training Area. The ferry is made up by four M3 amphibious rigs of 28 Amphibious Engineers. With Challenger 2 being a MLC 70 class vehicle, two M 3s are needed for one tank.

which is smaller than the Perkins engine of the Challenger 2, develops 1,500hp and in the gained space because of its reduced size, can house additional fuel tanks are mounted which raise the road range of the vehicle. Following factory information the capable power pack provides Challenger 2E with a top road speed of seventy-two kilometers-per-hour and a top cross-country speed of forty-two kilometers-per-hour. The power pack also contains a new air filtration and cooling system which allows a better performance in hot climactic conditions, such as deserts. The Challenger 2E was also fitted with a new integrated weapon control and battlefield management system. This includes a gyro-stabilized panoramic SAGEM MVS 580 day/thermal sight for the commander and SAGEM SAVAN 15 gyro-stabilized day/thermal sight for the gunner. This facilitates hunter/killer operations with a common engagement sequence. In the driver compartment a new power pack information panel was fitted, the steering was changed from tillers to a steering wheel and for night driving a thermal imaging night viewer was fitted. Instead of the turret roof mounted 7.62mm GPMG L7A2 for the loader Challenger 2E is fitted with a 12.7mm M2HB Browning machine gun for area defense. Together with the Challenger 2E a new APFSDS-T projectile with a conventional penetrator, unofficially designated L28 and using the L16 charge system, is offered to export customers who do not want to use the DU projectile.

Challenger 2E has been demonstrated in Greece and some states in the Middle East, but at the time of writing no customer has been announced. This may change after Challenger 2 performed well during the 2003 Gulf War. Challenger 2 and Challenger 2E both have plenty of growth potential—this may include an even more sophisticated fire data computer or a new 140mm gun. The Military Standard 1553 data bus and digital CDC computer of the Challenger 2 have the capacity to be connected with additional systems such as a Battlefield Information Control System and navigation and training systems.

2003 Gulf War Modifications

When British troops entered into Iraq during the opening first days of Operation "Iraqi Freedom," Challenger 2 MBTs of the Royal Scots Dragoon Guards, the 2nd Royal Tank Regiment and Queen's Royal Lancers went to war with a number of modifications from their initial design. Most of these improvements were carried out just before the war broke out and were based on the experience gathered by British tank troops during the "Saif Sareea 2" exercise held in Oman in autumn 2001. Modifications included fitting full length side skirts and additional mud flaps in order to minimize the amount of dust being thrown up. The engine filtration system was improved by special sand filters and an oil

Challenger 2 of the Royal Scots Dragoon Guards during exercise "Ulan Eagle 99" held on Drawsko Pomorski Training Area in Poland. Note the red desert rat insignia of the 7th Armoured Brigade painted on the TOGS of the tank.

Shown to advantage in this photograph are the Thermal Observation and Gunnery Sight II (TOGS II) over the gun, the commander's 360° traversal fully SFIM stabilized panoramic sight VS 580-10 mounted on the turret roof and the gunner's stabilized Gunner's Primary Sight to the right of the gun in front of the commander's sight. The vehicle is fitted with the direct fire weapons effect system (DFWES) and belongs to the Royal Scots Dragoon Guards.

From its well dug in position, a Challenger 2 of the Royal Scots Dragoon Guards over watch an engineer unit which is preparing defenses in the low ground in front of the tank's position. The picture was taken during exercise "Ulan Eagle 99" in Poland.

Skillfully camouflaged, these Challenger 2s from the Royal Scots Dragoon Guards were seen during exercise "Ulan Eagle 99" in Poland. The electric power system together with the vehicle batteries allow a crew of a Challenger 2 to observe the territory in front of them using the TOGS without running the engine for at least two hours.

temperature monitoring system was fitted to the engine. Challenger 2 MBTs deployed to Iraq, like those deployed to Kosovo and Bosnia, were fitted with the Dorchester Armour Level 2 appliqué armor kit. The kit consists of up-armored side plates which are mounted onto the side of the vehicle and a frame fitted to the top toe plate. In the frame Explosive Reactive Armour packs are mounted.

Conclusion

The Challenger 2 has provided the British Army with a state-of-the-art weapon system that surpasses the capabilities and vision of the Chieftain or Challenger 1. A unique advantage of the Challengers 2 is the very high first round hit capability of the weapon system with APFSDS ammunition even when moving. The Warrior infantry fighting vehicle and the Challenger 2 are both able to keep up in speed with the other, which allows British battle groups to operate with high speed on modern battle fields without one of the two combat arms being limited by the capabilities of the other. Increased silent watch capability, reliability, reduced crew fatigue due to ergonomic design, as well as the self deploy ability of Challenger 2 offer the British tank units and combined arms battle groups a high degree of flexibility and combat power on the modern battlefield.

Challenger 2 Technical Data

Crew:	4 soldiers: commander, driver, gunner and loader	Average cross country speed:	40 km/h
		Maximum gradient:	58%
Combat weight:	64 tons (including ammunition, fuel and kit of the crew, but not the crew)	Trench crossing:	2800mm
		Fording:	1070mm
		Power to weight ratio:	14kW/ton
Combat weight:	68.4 tons (combat weight plus Blade Earth Moving Attachment and side armor)	Engine:	Perkins Condor V 12 twin turbocharged diesel engine developing 1200bhp
Operation bridge classification:	MLC 70	Transmission:	David Brown TN 54 transmission with 6 forward and 2 reverse gears
Length:	11753mm (Gun in 12 o'clock position), 9806mm (Gun in 6 o'clock position)	Track:	Hydraulically adjusted double pin track, 650mm wide, made by William Cook Defence
Width	3922mm (With add on armor side skirts)	Suspension:	Hydrogas with variable spring rate
Height:	3038mm		
Width between tracks:	2170mm	Main armament.	120mm Royal Ordnance L30 rifled tank gun
Fuel capacity:	1942 litres (includes 2x 175 litres External Fuel Drums)	Secondary armament:	Coaxial machine gun: 7,62mm Hughes Chain Gun L94A1 Loaders machine gun: 7,62mm GPMG L7A2
Range:	550km on road or 300km cross country (with External Fuel Drums)		
Ground clearance:	512mm	Smoke Dischargers.	Exhaust smoke injection and two banks of 5 L8 smoke grenade dischargers
Vertical obstacle crossing:	900mm		
Maximum road speed:	59 km/h		

Challenger 2 MBT

The Challenger 2 is Britain's latest MBT battle tank and all armored regiments are equipped with it. The Challenger 2 saw first operational action with The Royal Scots Dragoon Guards in Kosovo in 2000. This picture was taken close to the boundary between Kosovo and Serbia during a patrol. All sixteen Challenger 2 of the SCOTS DG battle group were fitted with the side plates belonging to the Dorchester Armour Level 2 appliqué armor kit.

Units Equipped with Challenger 2

By April 2003, the British Army could field six armored regiments equipped with the Challenger 2 MBT. Each of these regiments field fifty-eight Challenger 2 MBTs divided among four squadrons with fourteen tanks each, while the remaining two tanks are part of the regiment's headquarters element. Each squadron has four tank troops with three tanks each and the squadron HQ with two more Challenger 2. The six Challenger 2 equipped regiments of the Royal Armored Corps include:

Royal Scots Dragoon Guards	based in Fallingbostel, Germany
2nd Royal Tank Regiment	based in Fallingbostel, Germany
Queen's Royal Lancers	based in Osnabrück, Germany
King's Royal Hussars	based in Tidworth, Great Britain
Queen's Royal Hussars	based in Sennelager, Germany
Royal Dragoon Guards	based in Münster, Germany

In addition to this impressive Challenger 2 force, the 1st Royal Tank Regiment, as part of the Land Warfare Component Battle Group at Warminster, fields A Squadron, 1RTR that is used as OPFOR during TESEX exercises. The rest of Regiment maintains one squadron equipped with Challenger 2 MBTs. 1RTR forms part of the joint NBC Regiment based at RAF Honington. The bulk of the remaining 24 Challenger 2 MBTs are stationed in Canada and belong to the vehicle park of the British Army Training Unit Suffield, while some are kept in depots as equipment reserve or are used for training by the Royal Armoured School in Bovington. In the future, the 2nd Royal Tank Regiment will be relocated to the United Kingdom, as the MoD has decided to give both of its major combat formations, the 1st Armoured Division (based in Germany) and the 3rd Armoured Division (based in the UK) a more equal level of firepower. The dislocation process is scheduled to be completed by 2004. It is also planned to replace the Queen's Royal Lancers by the Queen's Dragoon Guards which are currently equipped as an armored reconnaissance regiment. This then will leave only three Challenger 2 MBTs equipped regiments in Germany, one for each of the three brigades of the 1st Armoured Division.

During an attack of an armored battle group a Challenger 2 can be seen engaging an enemy position while moving. The vehicle is equipped with the direct fire weapons effect system (DFWES), consisting of active and passive sensors and used to simulate the effects of the Challenger 2's main gun, coaxial machine gun and laser range finder. In addition to the main gun also the coaxial 7.62mm L94A1 Chain Gun is stabilized and therefore can be used effectively during the move.

This top view of a Challenger 2 of the Royal Scots Dragoon Guards well illustrates the conventional layout of the MBT. The diver is situated to the front, the turret is placed in the center of the chassis and the engine compartment is located in the rear. Also well visible are the two rear-mounted 175-liters External Fuel Drums. The Challenger 2 chassis is basically the same as that of Challenger 1, but features 156 modifications from the original design. One of these modifications was the redesign of the engine compartment and engine decks.

A Challenger 2 MBT of the Royal Scots Dragoon Guards speeds up during a road move in Kosovo in 2000. Powered by a Perkins Condor V-12 twin turbocharged diesel engine which develops 1,200bhp Challenger 2 can reach a top road speed of 59 km/hr.

For area defense, a 7.62mm GPMG L7A2 machine gun is mounted on the gunner's side of the turret roof. The gas operated weapon has a combat range of up to 1,800 meters and a theoretical rate of fire of 625 to 750 rounds-per-minute. For the L7A2 and the Chain Gun L94A1, which both use the same ammunition, a total of 4,200 round are stored inside Challenger 2.

Next to the fully SFIM stabilized panoramic sight VS 580-10, a tank commander of the Royal Scots Dragoon Guards can be seen during a patrol in Kosovo early 2000. The commander is wearing the standard British Army combat vehicle crewman helmet with head set and microphone.

This picture shows a Challenger 2 with its business end. Above the 120mm L30 rifled tank gun the Thermal Observation and Gunnery Sight II (TOGS II) thermal imaging system can be seen. The sight is protected by an armored cover also comprising an armored door, which here is open to give view onto the sight.

Rear view of a Challenger 2 of an A Squadron 1st Royal Tank Regiment forming part of the Land Warfare Component Battle Group at Warminster. Note the two 175-liters External Fuel Drums at the vehicle's rear. The vehicle is painted in green and sand. A similar camouflage is applied to the Challenger 2 stationed at the British Army Training Unit Suffield (BATUS).

During the Army 2002 fire power demonstration, a Challenger 2 of Land Warfare Component Battle Group at Warminster engages a simulated enemy armored column. The vehicle belongs to A Squadron 1st Royal Tank Regiment. The 55 caliber 120mm L30 rifled tank gun of Challenger 2 can fire APFSDS-T, HESH and Smoke projectiles as well as the newly developed L27A1 APFSDS Depleted Uranium (DU) round of the CHARM 3 system.

Challenger 2 MBTs of A Squadron 1st Royal Tank Regiment taking part in the Army 2002 demonstration. Note the famous "Chinese Eyes" badge painted to the front on the side of the turret. 1RTR took over the "Chinese Eyes" from 4RTR when both regiments amalgamated in the mid-1990s. Within the Royal Tank Regiment the tradition to paint "Chinese Eyes" onto tanks dates back to 1917. It was then that Mr. Yew Tong Sen, a Chinese businessman, gave a substantial sum of money to allow the purchase of new tanks. After being shown the tanks Mr. Yew Tong Sen insisted that they should have their own eyes to see their way in adversity.

The Challenger 2 MBTs of the Land Warfare Component Battle Group at Warminster are painted in a camouflage pattern of dark green and sand. The reason for this is that the LWBG is used as OPFOR during TESEX exercises and a different camouflage pattern for the enemy makes the exercise more realistic and identification of enemy troops a bit easier.

During a live firing exercise on Salisbury Plain a Challenger 2 of A Squadron 1st Royal Tank Regiment shows his mobility. With a combat weight of 64 tons Challenger 2 reaches an average cross country speed of 40 km/hr.

During the Army 2002 fire power demonstrations, a tank troop of A Squadron 1st Royal Tank Regiment can be seen engaging enemy positions in support of battle group attack. Within the British armored regiments each tank troop consists of three Challenger 2 MBTs. With a well trained crew and under ideal circumstances by the use of the "Hunter Killer System" a Challenger 2 is able to hit up to six targets in a remarkable thirty seconds.

This Challenger 2 MBT of D Squadron Queen's Royal Hussars was pictured during exercise "Ulan Eagle 2000" in Poland. The vehicle is equipped with the direct fire weapons effect system (DFWES), consisting of active and passive sensors. Made by Saab in Sweden and known in company terms as the BT 46. DFWES simulates the effects of the Challenger 2's main gun, coaxial machine gun and laser range finder.

After a Challenger 2 has engaged his target the fume extractor can be seen at work. The fume extractor prevents that burned powder gasses enter the fighting compartment. The number on the rear of the turret identifies the vehicle as the third tank of the fourth troop. The first tank is that of the troop commander bearing a "40" and the second tank is a gun tank bearing "41." The vehicle belongs to A Squadron 1RTR.

A Challenger 2 of D Squadron Queen´s Royal Hussars at full speed. Challenger 2 is powered by a Perkins Condor V 12 twin turbocharged diesel engine which develops 1,200bhp. The engine is coupled to a David Brown TN 54 transmission with six forward and two reverse gears. The power pack of Challenger 2 allows the vehicle to reach a top speed of 59 km/hr while traveling on roads or 40 km/hr while traveling cross country.

During exercise "Ulan Eagle 2000" held in Poland on Drawsko Pomorski Training Area here two Challenger 2 of D Squadron Queen´s Royal Hussars can be seen driving onto an M3 ferry.

During an exercise break here the tanks of D Squadron the Queen´s Royal Hussars can be seen lined up on Drawsko Pomorski Training Area in 2000. A Challenger 2 tank squadron consists of 14 Challenger 2 divided among four troops of three tanks and two tanks in the squadron HQ. A Challenger 2 equipped regiment of the British Army can field four such squadrons. Two additional tanks in the regimental HQ bring the total number of tanks in a single regiment to fifty-eight.

By injecting engine oil into its exhaust system Challenger 2 can generate a smoke screen for protection when detected by enemy armor. In addition to the smoke generation system the tank is fitted with two banks of five smoke grenade dischargers mounted on either side of the turret. With these L8A4 smoke grenades can be fired, being electrically triggered by the crew from under armor. The L8A4 produces a phosphorous smoke screen which offers protection from detection by enemy surveillance devices operating in visual and near infra red wave bands.

A tank commander of the Queen's Royal Hussars can here be seen posing for the camera standing in his cupola. In front of him the commander's fully SFIM stabilized panoramic sight VS 580-10 can be seen. The turret mounted sight has a magnification of x3.2 and x10.5 by day and contains an Nd-YAG laser range finder. The sight can be traversed 360° has an elevation range from minus +/- 35 degrees.

Here a tank troop from D Squadron the Queen's Royal Hussars can be seen advancing while using dead ground. Each tank troop can field three Challenger 2 MBTs, four troops form a company. In the squadron there are two additional Challenger 2 MBTs used in the squadron HQ. In the rear the first tank of another troop can be seen.

A Challenger 2 of the Royal Scots Dragoon Guards seen at the boundary between Kosovo and Serbia in March 2000. Note that the vehicle is partly camouflaged with winter camouflage netting. Depending on the role of a tank within the regiment a vehicle might be fitted with the standard two VRC 353 Clansman radios if it is a gun tank or with a more sophisticated mix of three radios if it is a command tank used by squadron or regimental commanders. Challenger 2 is fitted with a Battle Management System (BMS) which provides crews and commanders with real live updates on the tactical situation via secure communication. In addition BMS can be used to transmit orders, requests and reports.

A Challenger 2 of the Royal Scots Dragoon Guards on patrol during the unit's Kosovo deployment with KFOR in 2001. The vehicle is fitted with the Dorchester Armour Level 2 appliqué armor kit comprising passive armor side plates and explosive reactive armor on the front. The front armor consists of a frame which is fitted to the toe plate and is fitted with Explosive Reactive Armor packs.

Rear-view of a Challenger 2 of the Royal Scots Dragoon Guards on patrol in Kosovo in 2001. Note the two 175-liters External Fuel Drums at the vehicle's rear. During live firing trials it was found out that the external fuel drums do not provide any hazard for the tank when being hit. The results of the trials which involved 7.62mm, HESH and DS(T) ammunition lead to the fact that there is no system on Challenger 2 with which the drums can be quickly released.

A pair of Challenger 2 MBT of the Royal Scots Dragoon Guards picks up speed during a patrol in Kosovo in 2001. Both tanks are fitted with the Dorchester Armour Level 2 appliqué armor kit comprising passive armor side plates and explosive reactive armor on the front.

A "Blade Earth Moving Attachment" (BEMA) can be mounted to the front of the Challenger 2. With a BEMA and add-on side armor Challenger 2 has a combat weight of 68.4 tons. Usually one tank in a squadron is fitted with a BEMA in order to provide the squadron commander with his own engineer capability. The BEMA can be used to dig tank scrapes or remove obstacles. The Pearson Combat Dozer UDK-1 can be seen fitted to a Challenger 2, as well. All Challenger 2s of the Omani and UK armed forces are prepared to take the UDK-1 without extra modification. The UDK-1 has a weight of 2,200 kilograms and a cutting depth of 175mm, fitting it to a Challenger 2 takes the crew approximately ten minutes.

A photograph of the Blade Earth Moving Attachment (BEMA) Pearson Combat Dozer UDK1 fitted to a Challenger 2 MBT. The BEMA can carry out bulldozing tasks such as ground leveling, digging, urban obstacle clearance and filling anti-tank ditches. The UDK-1 incorporates a hydraulic power pack into the boom arm and is thus a totally self-contained unit. A wedge-block mounting system enables the bulldozer to be removed from one vehicle and fitted to another tank in less than fifteen minutes. The bulldozer fits directly to the glacis plate by means of attaching two anchor blocks and attachment eyes pre-welded to the glacis plate. Electrical connection is made between a harness fitted permanently to the bulldozer and a glacis plate harness. The harness passes through armored ducting to a control box in the driver's compartment. The UDK-1 unit comprises a blade and boom fitted to a mounting plate, with the blade position controlled by a hydraulic cylinder and top link. The blade is a fabricated steel unit fitted with replaceable hardened steel cutting edges and corner tips. The shown blade is fitted with an extension in the center that increases dozing capacity and reduces spillage. The control box in the drive's compartment controls blade lift and lowering functions electrically, using a joystick lever.

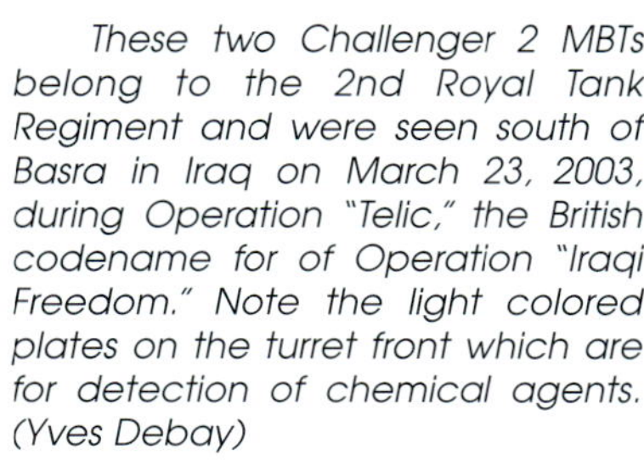

These two Challenger 2 MBTs belong to the 2nd Royal Tank Regiment and were seen south of Basra in Iraq on March 23, 2003, during Operation "Telic," the British codename for of Operation "Iraqi Freedom." Note the light colored plates on the turret front which are for detection of chemical agents. (Yves Debay)

A total of 120 Challenger 2s from the 7th Armoured Brigade saw action during the fighting in Iraq in March and April 2003. A pair of Challenger 2 MBTs of the Royal Scots Dragoon Guards can be seen in action twenty-kilometers south of Basra on the morning of the March 23. The vehicles are fitted with the side and front add-on armor package. Among other modifications the full length side skirts can be well seen. (Yves Debay)

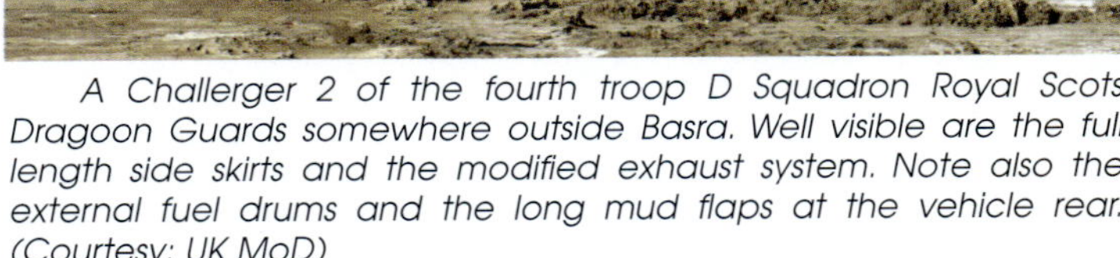

A Challerger 2 of the fourth troop D Squadron Royal Scots Dragoon Guards somewhere outside Basra. Well visible are the full length side skirts and the modified exhaust system. Note also the external fuel drums and the long mud flaps at the vehicle rear. (Courtesy: UK MoD)

During the capture of Basra Challenger 2 of the Royal Scots Dragoon Guards worked closely together with Cobra attack helicopters of the USMC. Note that the vehicle is bearing the typical arrowhead markings used by US forces to identify units and vehicles inside brigades and divisions. (Courtesy: UK MoD)

After the city of Basra fell into the hands of the coalition forces, here a Challenger 2 of the Royal Scots Dragoon Guards can be seen placed as a sentry on a large crossroads. During the capture of Basra Challenger 2 main battle tanks supported Royal Marine Commandos against enemy armored vehicles several times. Note the BV-206 of the Royal Marine Commandos in the back. (Courtesy: UK MoD)

Side-view of the very same Challenger 2 of the Royal Scots Dragoon Guards. Note the U.S. Army style arrow markings which are usually used to identify the unit to which a vehicle belongs. The vehicle is fitted with the side and front add-on armor package, full length side skirts and the modified exhaust system. (Yves Debay)

This vehicle belongs to the Royal Scots Dragoon Guards and was seen in the outskirts of Basra, Iraq on April 15, 2003. Note the coaxial 7.62mm L 94A1 Chain Gun which is situated to the right of the 120mm 55 caliber L30 rifled tank gun on the Challenger 2 MBT. (Yves Debay)

During Operation "Telic" all Challenger 2 MBTs of the 7th Armoured Brigade were fitted with the side and front add-on armor package. The vehicle belongs to the Royal Scots Dragoon Guards and was seen in the outskirts of Basra in Iraq on April 15. Note the green hand smoke grenade strapped to the commander's stabilized panoramic sight. (Yves Debay)

A mechanized platoon from the 1-18 Infantry Battalion mans a temporary checkpoint in the northern sector of the Alpha Bowl at the Combat Maneuver Training Center. The Bradley's weapon systems, along with the individual weapons, are loaded with blank training ammunition. A Bradley crew must be prepared to handle peace support tasks along with their traditional combat role.

"Hold the line," shouted the platoon leaders down the main street of "Cernice". With much effort and continuous struggle, members of the 1-18th Infantry attempted to hold back a large group of demonstrators to prevent them from overtaking their command post within the town. The mob yelled obscenities and anti-American slogans at the American troops, but the soldiers remained calm despite the mob's continued provocation. The leader of the mob directed the group of demonstrators to continue the shouting and pushing. Stones and rocks began to fly and in short time injuries resulted on both sides. One by one officers of the American unit pointed out the troublemakers, and they were quickly grabbed and arrested.

This scenario was not taking place in Kosovo, but rather at U.S. Army Europe's 7th Army Training Command, Combat Maneuver Training Center in Hohenfels, Germany, and was part of Mountain Guardian VII/02, an exercise to prepare the 2d Brigade Combat Team (Dagger), 1st Infantry Division ("Big Red One"), for their deployment to Kosovo. The twenty-day exercise followed a detailed script of events, called Complex Battlefield Incidents, similar to the one mentioned above, that tested the Brigade's capability to deal with situations they most probably would face in Kosovo.

KFOR Deployment Preparation

The U.S. Army supports the NATO peacekeeping mission in Kosovo by rotating out to that country a Brigade Combat Team (BCT) every six months. The majority of the teams are from U.S. Army Europe (USAREUR) units comprising the 1st Infantry Division ("Big Red One") and the 1st Armored Division ("Old Ironsides").

Three months prior to each BCT deployment, the units go through an intense training exercise at the Combat Maneuver Training Center (CMTC) in Hohenfels. In 2002, two BCTs from 1st ID were scheduled for KFOR duty. From 17 February to 17 March 2002, the 2d "Dagger" Brigade Combat Team out of Schweinfurt completed their preparation for KFOR duty during Exercise "Mountain Guardian VII/02" in Hohenfels. The exercise involved over 5000 soldiers – about 4200 from various units of the 2d "Dagger" Brigade, 230 soldiers of the 1-4 Infantry Battalion (OPFOR), 300 soldiers from the Observer Controller Teams of CMTC, and 450 specially selected civilian "actors", or Civilians on the Battlefield (COBs).

Kosovo Replication in Bavaria, Germany

Mountain Guardian VII/02 provided realistic training across the entire spectrum of conflict, using scenarios developed from the most recent KFOR operations. The BCT faced a wide range of situations, from dealing with local citizens to actual conflict, while providing Stability and Support Operations (SASO) along the three-mile Kosovo safety zone. Mountain Guardian VII/02 was U.S. Army Europe's most expensive exercise, costing the U.S. government over $10M. The high cost resulted from turning the Combat Maneuver Training Center in Hohenfels into a mini-Kosovo complete with towns, mosques, cities, and even base camps like Camp "Bondsteel" and Camp "Montieth".

Mission Rehearsal Exercise (MRE)

A Bradley Fighting Vehicle Team is trained to perform in combat situations. However, during Mountain Guardian VII/02, these teams faced unfamiliar tasks such as breaking up a demonstration and defusing a hostile crisis. The exercise script was designed to test soldiers' skills by providing a constant bombardment of varied, worst-case scenarios the soldiers could expect to face on their "worst day" in Kosovo. For example, in one town the unit had to call for a Black Hawk helicopter to evacuate a local citizen who was severely injured after being struck by a military vehicle.

"Regulators" of the 527th Military Police (MP) Company. Military Police companies are outfitted with a full spectrum of lethal and non-lethal weapons for their mission in Kosovo. Here soldiers of the 527th MP Company wear Riot Control Equipment, which includes face shields, protective shields, shin guards, and a riot baton.

A 527th MP Company platoon leader, shown here outfitted in Riot Control Gear and armed with a M4 carbine fitted with a 40mm grenade launcher. A component of the MILES II training system is attached to the barrel of the weapon.

A Military Police dog and handler. German Shepherds play an important role in assisting Military Police with apprehensions and the search of buildings.

Other events included reported rapes, arrests of war criminals, escorting ethnic groups back to their homes, assisting the international police (UNMIK), or the emergency landing of a helicopter between two zones of responsibility. The soldiers quickly learned that making an incorrect decision escalated the situation or had consequences later on in the exercise. Tense moments often burst into full-scale simulated riots, which tested the soldiers' abilities to maintain a cool demeanor while responding decisively.

Scripted Exercise

As stated above, Mountain Guardian VII/02 consisted of scripted events that occurred constantly throughout each day of the exercise. Over 1200 of these events, or Complex Battle Incidents, took place during MG VII/02. Each event was tied to one of the four critical training objectives for the Brigade. These tasks included security and peacekeeping operations, coordination with international authorities and organizations, local and secret elections, and controlling the border conflict between Yugoslavian and rebel forces.

A team of military personnel, government officials, contracted personnel, and experienced SASO personnel worked together to develop the exercise scenarios to meet the Division Commander's training intent. Monitoring the exercise were members of the Combat Maneuver Training Center's Observer Controller (O/C) Teams, who assisted the units to

On the eve of the offensive against Iraq in 1992, a New York Times reporter asked Major General McGaffrey, the former Commander of the 24th U.S. Infantry Division, "What is the most important weapon system for this war?" He answered, "Damn good trucks!" A wide variety of support vehicles are needed to get a Brigade Combat Team to the battle. The 5-ton trucks, series M939, replaced the old M35 series trucks in 1992. The M109A3 Shop Van is the only version still used today. The 299th SPT (Forward Support Battalion) of the 1st Infantry Division uses the M109A3 as a rolling workshop and spare parts warehouse. The first released version of the M109 had five side windows, and the body was mounted on a single rail frame. The newer version, the M109A2/A3, has a double-railed frame and only three side windows.

A M925 5-ton truck from the 299th Forward Support Battalion is seen here near Camp "Montieth" in the fictional city of Kittensee in the Combat Maneuver Training Center, Hohenfels, Germany. This 5-ton vehicle is outfitted with a M2 HM machine gun, which is used for additional security and cover fire during convoy operations. Also of note are the standard front tire treads and the front-mounted winch. The designation "M923" is for models without the winch. The 14.6-ton M925 is powered by a 6-cylinder Cummings diesel motor, model NHC 250, which puts out 250 horsepower with a top speed of 72k/h (45 mph).

A series M923 truck, developed from the 5-ton M809. The 299th(FSB) uses this M923 as a carrier for the mechanics workshop. In comparison to the older M809 series, the M923 has a larger driver's compartment and reduced noise output. The M923s are powered by a 240-hp Cummings NHC 250, a 6-cylinder diesel motor with an Allison automatic transmission. A common feature of the M923A2 5-ton truck is the single-wheeled, 14.0R20 tires and the Central Inflation System. Due to this large wheel size, the M923A2 has earned the nickname "Big Foot".

HMMWV maintenance in Camp "Magrath". The M936 wrecker is used to transport light- to medium-sized wheeled vehicles. The Oshkosh M984A1 HEMMT Recovery Truck replaces the M939 wrecker in combat. The crane of the M936 is rated at 4536 kilograms (10,002lb) and can rotate 270 degrees. Like the M923 and the M923A2, the M936 wrecker belongs to the series M939 family of vehicles.

achieve their training goals by ensuring realistic, challenging and safe training, using doctrinally correct informal and formal After Action Reviews, and through teaching, coaching, and mentoring unit leaders. Exercise Controllers used feedback provided by the O/C teams daily to alter CBI events based on the outcome of previous CBI events. Each CBI had several story line paths based on how the unit handled each situation. For example, if a unit failed to find explosives located in a car during a vehicle check, that car might be used later on in the exercise in a car-bombing CBI event. However, if the unit did find the explosives then another story line would be followed.

Soldiers came face-to-face with a diverse cast of characters designed to test their peacekeeping skills. Civilians on the Battlefield (COBs) have played an important role since the first Mountain Guardian exercise at the Combat Maneuver Training Center. Over 400 COBs, consisting of mostly local nationals, were hired for Mountain Guardian VII/02 to portray local civilians, government officials, religious officials, news media, rebel forces, and members of foreign military forces. Each of the COBs was assigned their own identity, complete with name and biography. The use of civilians helped replicate the Kosovo environment and provided for realistic training events such as late-night house fires, domestic disputes, terrorist attacks, and altercations between ethnic groups. The hired COBs,

The standard model of the Oshkosh M977 HEMMT truck is a cargo truck with a Material Handling Crane mounted on the rear. The M977 is a well-designed multi-function vehicle operable on virtually any type of terrain. The 8x8 HEMMT is powered by a 445-horsepower, 8-cylinder Detroit 8V-92T diesel motor, and can reach a maximum speed of 89k/h (55 mph) with a full 27-ton load. This 10-ton HEMMT belongs to the 9th Engineer Brigade and is used to transport the Mine Clearing Line Charge System (MICLIC). The MICLIC is used to open a line through a minefield.

One difference between this M1075 Palletized Load System (PLS) truck and the version M1074 PLS is that the M1075 is equipped with a loading crane manufactured by Grove. The improved M1075 PLS model also has the advantage of having all the loading arm controls located within the driver's cab, which allows for rapid on/off loading of supplies in less than one minute without leaving the cab of the truck.

The Oshkosh M984A1 is the successor to the M936 wrecker. The rear tow bar can carry light tracked vehicles (from M113 series) weighing up to 24 tons. The Grove Material Handling Crane (MHC) mounted on the rear of the vehicle has a maximum towing capacity of 2724kg (6000 pounds) and can easily lift tank engines. The recovery winch of the M984A1 has a length of 67 meters (220 feet) and has a line pull of 18 tons.

The mission of the Mechanized Infantry Platoon using the four M2A2ODS (Operation Desert Storm) Bradley Fighting Vehicles took on a different role during Mountain Guardian VII/02. Instead of its normal combat role, the Bradley was used as a patrol vehicle, a Quick Reaction Force (QRF) transport vehicle, and as a static and mobile security vehicle. The photo shows a M2A2 ODS Bradley from 1-18 Infantry Battalion patrolling through the town of Kittensee. To the right of the Bradley is a HMMWV from the Warhog Observer Controller Team.

A M2A2ODS Bradley from 1st Platoon, Bravo Company, 1st Battalion, 187th Infantry Regiment "Blue Spaders" seen here receiving repairs near the Kirchenoedenhart ruins in Hohenfels. All weapons systems remain in the "ready" state while mechanics work on the engine.

ranging in age from the young to the elderly, came primarily from Germany and neighboring countries such as Hungary. They worked and lived in both the maneuver area and on the Hohenfels installation for the duration of the exercise.

Summary

The Operation Group of the Combat Maneuver Training Center provided an optimal training environment during Mountain Guardian VII/02 in preparing the 2d "Dagger" Brigade for their deployment to Kosovo. Soldiers faced situations that they rarely see in their normal day-to-day Army training. They departed with a better understanding of the environment into which they were deploying, from mine threats to the ethnic tension, to the peacekeeping tasks, to the potential for all out conflict. They were able to practice skills essential to stability and support operations such as negotiations, demonstrating patience and working with national-level government officials. Their staffs had the opportunity to iron out procedures for tracking Task Force operations on a daily basis. Their training at CMTC was extremely beneficial and fully prepared them to face the "worst day" in Kosovo.

In November 2002, the 2d "Dagger" Brigade's Kosovo mission would have ended. They would be replaced by the 3d "Iron Knight" Brigade Combat Team of the 1st Infantry Division, who completed their exercise (Mountain Guardian VII/03) in September.

M1117 ASV (Armored Security Vehicle)

The M1117 ASV (Armored Security Vehicle) had its premiere showing in Germany during exercise Mountain Guardian VII/02. The vehicle, fielded by the 18th Military Police Brigade, is used by Brigade Army elements and provides better armor protection and firepower than the HMMVW police patrol vehicle. The Army plans to outfit every MP Company with 12 ASVs distributed evenly over four platoons. An ASV patrol group would consist of two HMMWVs and one ASV, which would provide cover and protection for the patrol. In Kosovo, the vehicles would be stationed in the two base camps (Bondsteel and Montieth).

Fielding by the U.S. Army and Air Force Military Police

The U.S. Army adopted the M1117 ASV as a wheeled armored vehicle in 2000. Manufactured by Textron Marine and Land Systems, the ASV was selected as the unit that will protect U.S. soldiers well into the next century, with the capability to fulfill multiple roles within the Army's mission. Corps-level Military Police companies received the first ASVs at the end of 2000. The Air Force has also shown interest in the ASV, with its version being called the Mobile Disrupter System (MODS). This version will include a high-energy laser used to destroy duds or other unwanted items found on an airfield.

A M2A2ODS Bradley scout from the 1-26 Infantry Battalion. A Bradley must be ready to support a defensive role as well as hold a position during peacekeeping operations. The TOW2A (Tube-launched, Optically Tracked, Wire Guided Rocket) has an effective range of over 3.2km (2 miles). The TOW of this Bradley sports the "Big Red One" symbol of the 1st Infantry Division.

The 1st Battalion, 7th Field Artillery "First Lightning" Regiment is part of the Division Artillery of the 1st Infantry Division. The Battalion is a subordinate element of the 2d "Dagger" Brigade Combat Team and during MG VII/02, M109A6 Paladins of the 1-7 Field Artillery provided direct fire support to the BCT. It is common practice within the 1-7 FA to stencil the name of famous battles on their gun tubes. Here the crew has chosen "Battle of the Bulge".

The "Iron Hammers" of the 2d "Dagger" Brigade Combat Team are the M1A1HA Abrams tanks belonging to the 1-77 Armor Regiment. During SASO operations, the Abrams serves as protection at checkpoints and is also used during patrols. Some also are positioned in the forward operations camps as part of reactionary forces. The Abrams in this photo is outfitted with an Israeli RAMTA Track-Width Mine Plow for breeching mine obstacles.

The M60AVLB (Armored Vehicle-Launched Bridge) is used for launching and retrieving a 60-foot scissors-type bridge. Designed for combat support, the AVLB is used in SASO operations to replace destroyed bridges and assist in getting humanitarian supplies to cut-off areas. Every U.S. Army Combat Engineer Battalion has four M60AVLBs per company. This AVLB belongs to the 9th Combat Engineer Battalion, otherwise known as the "Gila Monsters".

"Roadblock". An M88A1 Medium Recovery Vehicle from HHC, 1-77 Armor Regiment, blocks the entrance to the Forward Operating Base in "Cernice".

Scouts from the 1-77 Armor Regiment conduct patrols along the three-mile "neutral-zone" during Mountain Guardian VII/02. Patrols are conducted using a minimum of four HMMWVs with various weapons configurations. This M1206, a special weapons-platform HMMWV, is equipped with a M240B machine gun and a front-mounted self-recovery winch.

Patrol scout HMMVWs carry a variety of equipment such as, tow bars, concertina wire, gas canisters, MREs, water jugs, ammunition, and anti-tank weapons. Even a digital camera is part of the standard equipment used here to photograph a "nosy" photojournalist.

An anti-aircraft "Avenger" weapons system, from Delta Battery (Delta Dawgs) of the 4th Battalion, 3d Air Defense Artillery, stands watch at a remote guard post. The four rocket tubes hold FIM-92C Stinger surface-to-air missiles. Installed under the tubes is a 12.7mm M3P machine gun. This Avenger HMMWV is also equipped with Identification Friend or Foe (IFF) door and rear panels as well as the MILE II Training System. The Avenger is deployed in division rear and echelons above division.

Several local translators will be assisting patrols of the 1-18 Infantry. In Kosovo, translators are contracted through a civilian firm by the U.S. State Department. Here an Observer/Controller from the Operations Group at CMTC observes the interaction between soldiers and a translator of a scripted event during MG VII/02.

Members of the 527th Military Police Company assist the international police (UNMIK) in keeping peace and harmony within a small village where ethnic tension has arisen. The UNMIK are assisting local police agencies in establishing law and order.

One of the typical Complex Battlefield Incidents (CBI) events during Mountain Guarding VII/02 was the escalating conflict with Yugoslavian forces along the three-mile neutral zone. Members of the "Vilslakian National Army" man this checkpoint along the "Yugoslavian border". This Vilslakian soldier, who is armed with a mock AK-47, is played by a soldier from the 1-4 Infantry (OPFOR) Battalion.

Mock demonstration. Members of the 1-18 Infantry attempt to control the situation after citizens of "Cernice" began a violent demonstration following the "death" of one of their townsfolk. The mob consists of hired actors controlled by the Civilian on the Battlefield team of the Combat Maneuver Training Center.

MEDEVAC in Kittensee! As part of the training event, an Army truck in the village of Kittensee hit a civilian. Due to the extent of his injuries, a Black Hawk UH-60Q MEDEVAC helicopter was quickly called to evacuate the "casualty" to a treatment facility. This Black Hawk is equipment with the External Stores Support System with attached external 220-gallon fuel tanks.

The motto "Eye of Death" has been painted on the side of this 1-4 Infantry (OPFOR) Battalion HMMWV that is camouflaged in a non-standard U.S. Army scheme. This M998 of the OPFOR Reconnaissance Platoon replicates a Yugoslavian scout vehicle. Note the use of the VISMOD (Visual Modification) device on the front of the vehicle and the Yugoslavian National Flag in the windshield.

A Black Hawk helicopter assists in an aero medical evacuation. The UH-60Q provides a six-patient litter system, on-board oxygen generation, and a medical suction system. The UH-60Q is a UH-60A derivative that incorporates approximate UH-60A characteristics.

On the main road through Kittensee, a medic from the Black Hawk performs first aid and prepares the casualty for transport.

The OH-58D Kiowa Warrior is the main observation/scout helicopter used by the 2d "Dagger" Brigade Combat Team. The supporting "birds" belong to the 1-4 Cavalry Regiment (nicknamed "Quarter Horse"). This Kiowa emergency-landed directly on the sector border of the 1-18 Infantry and the 1-77 Armor Regiments. Shortly after the distress call, a search and rescue team from 2-1 AVN appeared on the scene in a Black Hawk helicopter to provide assistance.

The crew of the Kiowa OH-58 helicopter inspects their "bird" for possible damage after conducting an emergency landing. The available weapons systems for the Kiowa Warrior include Air-to-Air Stinger (ATAS) and Air-to-Ground (ATG) Hellfire missiles, 2.75-inch rockets, and a .50 caliber machine gun. The Mass-Mounted Sight (MMS) on top of the aircraft contains a television camera, laser sight, and Forward Looking Infrared (FLIR) system. To sight on a target, the aircraft simply rises above cover (trees, hilltop) just enough to expose only the ball of the MMS.

The M1117 ASV (Armored Security Vehicle) saw its first action in Germany during the Mountain Guardian VII/02 exercise. This ASV belongs to the 527th Military Police Company of the 18th MP Brigade. Like all other vehicles participating in the exercise, this one is equipped with the MILES II Laser Engagement System.

The crew of a Guardian consists of a gunner, vehicle commander and driver, and they wear olive-colored NOMEX fireproof suits and the Combat Vehicle Crewman Helmet (CVC) with integrated intercom system.

The mission of the M1117 ASV Guardian is to support the expanding Military Police mission during Security and Support Operations. In addition, the ASV serves as a security escort vehicle for high-ranking officials, as displayed here during General Montgomery Meigs' (Commanding General United States Army Europe) visit to Exercise "Mountain Guardian VII".

The M1117 ASV operates with two HMMWVs in a MP squad during patrols. The ASV provides cover fire for the two HMMWVs during enemy contact.

M1117 "Guardian"
Armored Security Vehicle

Ralph Zwilling

On 30 March 1999, after a series of intensive tests, the U.S. Army Tank Automotive & Armaments Command ordered 96 Armored Security Vehicles valued at $50 Million. In August 2000, the 18th MP Brigade was issued the first six series vehicles of the ASV M1117 Guardian, which were handed over to the 615th MP Company in Vilseck, Germany and the 527th MP Company in Giessen, Germany.

Introduction

For many years, the High Mobility Multipurpose Wheeled Vehicle (HMMWV) has been the standard vehicle of the U.S. Military Police battalions. The knowledge gained during missions over the past years has allowed the U.S. Army to develop a new wheeled vehicle for the Military Police. Mainly, the HMMWV showed clear shortcomings in the area of armor protection and armament, problems that had to be overcome. As the new Armored Security Vehicle (ASV) will mostly be used in peacekeeping and peacemaking operations, high importance was placed on improving crew protection, and increasing cargo space and firepower. The ASV offers exceptional crew protection through the employment of a modular expandable armor system (MEXAS), which was developed by the German Ingenieurbüro Deisenroth (IBD). MEXAS consists of ceramic composite appliqué armor on the exterior surfaces and a spall liner in the interior.

The U.S. Army Europe's 18th MP Brigade received the first of its M1117 Guardian Armored Security Vehicles in August 2000. This ASV of the 527th MP Company, 709th MP Battalion from Giessen, Germany took part in Mission Rehearsal Exercise "Mountain Guardian VII" in the CMTC-Hohenfels in March 2002. Note the MILES II Laser Engagement System on the Upgunned Weapon Station (UGWS).

By going through the access hatch at the rear of the vehicle and passing through a tunnel, which is also used as a stowage area, one can reach the crew compartment in the front of the vehicle. Note the fuel can, the Central Tire Inflation System (CTIS) and the bumper codes.

The armament of the ASV M1117 consists of the Upgunned Weapon Station (UGWS) with a Browning .50 caliber M48 Turret Mounted Machine Gun and a Rock Island Arsenal 40mm Mk.19 Mod 3 Grenade Machine Gun. Note the SINCGARS antenna at the rear of the vehicle and the strobe light above the .50 caliber gun barrel on the UGWS.

The two access hatches in the middle of the hull have firing ports that enable the troops inside to fire their weapons under armor protection. Note the cap of the right fuel tank at the front of the ASV and the Velcro strips of the MILES II laser engagement system on the turret.

This advanced armor offers front, rear and side protection from .50 caliber armor-piercing ammunition. The ASV is also protected from 12-pound mine blasts under each wheel and from 155mm artillery shell fragments detonated at 15 meters (49 feet) overhead.

During the humanitarian operations that took place over the last several years, the Military Police have not only practiced police missions but also moved casualties and large quantities of supplies to faraway regions. To meet these demands, the ASV was designed to carry payloads of up to 1.5 tons. In 1995, Textron Marine & Land Systems was awarded an EMD contact to produce four prototype vehicles. This contract contained additional production options that could potentially increase the quantity ordered to 250. On 30 March 1999, following intensive tests, the U.S. Army Tank Automotive & Armaments Command ordered 96 Armored Security Vehicles with a value of $50 Million. One of the four handmade prototypes was destroyed in testing and the remaining three were sent back to TM&LS to be refurbished.

Fielding of the M1117s

In August 2000, the 18th MP Brigade was issued the first six series vehicles of the M1117 Guardian (No. 5-10), which were handed over to the 615th MP Company in Vilseck and the 527th MP Company in Giessen. After the four-week training for the crews in the Grafenwöhr Training Area was completed, one platoon from each of the two MP companies was equipped with the ASV and deployed to Kosovo. In January, the next six vehicles (No. 11-13 and the three refurbished vehicles) were sent directly to Kosovo to join with MP Task Force 793. In June 2001, the units and all of the 12 ASVs left Kosovo and returned to Germany.

During the summer of 2001, the 66th MP Company, 504th MP Battalion from Fort Lewis, Washington was issued the next 12 ASVs. They deployed to Kosovo with their vehicles in November 2001. These M1117s were left in Kosovo to become part of Task Force Falcon's property. MP Task Force 709, who is now using the 12 ASVs, was recently deployed to Kosovo. The 18th MP Brigade is not scheduled to receive their next 12 vehicles until late 2003 or early 2004. Since the fielding in Fort Lewis, another 12 M1117s have been fielded to the Military Police at Fort Hood, Texas.

There has been some misleading information published in the American press saying that the ASV program has been cancelled. For the time being, additional funding has been cancelled, but the first 96 vehicles have already been paid for and will continue to come off the production line until 2004 or 2005. Prior to that time, the MP School will decide whether to request further funding for the remaining vehicles that are required. At the moment there is some talk of fielding the new Stryker vehicle to MPs instead. The concerns of many Military Police soldiers are that the Stryker is larger, heavier and not as well suited to the MP mission. They also cost over $2 million each while an ASV costs closer to $500,000 each.

Technical Performance

The technical performance of the new M1117 armored wheeled vehicle of the U.S. Military Police is amazing. The 260hp 6-cylinder Cummins 6CTA 8.3 diesel engine, with its 8.3-liter (2.2-gallon) displacement, exhaust turbo charger and inter-cooling (which is also used in the M939 truck series), provides the 13.4-ton vehicle with a maximum speed of 100km/h (62 mph). Acceleration from 0 to 32km/h (20 mph) takes no longer than seven seconds. The fuel tank has a capacity of 189 liters (50 gallons). Situated in front of the crew compartment, it provides a cruising range of up to 708km (440 miles).

The engine and the transmission are both in the left rear of the M1117 Guardian. The Allison MD 3560 automatic transmission, which offers six forward gears and one reverse gear, in combination with the fully independent suspension with coil springs, Rockwell R-611 axles, and Michelin 14.00 R20XZL tires with "run flat" inserts, give the M1117 outstanding mobility on roads and in heavy terrain. Because of its high ground clearance of 46cm (18 inches), vertical obstacles up to a height of 60cm (24 inches) and trenches up to a width of 50cm (20 inches) are no problem for the ASV. Additionally, it can cross water obstacles up to a depth of 1.52m (5 feet) without preparation.

The M1117 Guardian is steered with hydraulic-power-assisted TRW Model TAS-65 steering. Like the M939 series 5-ton truck, the ASV has a Central Tire Inflation System (CITS) that is controlled from the driver's station. CTIS is designed to work automatically in case of tire leakage. Additionally, to protect valves, CTIS will adjust tire pressure when a road

The exhaust pipe of the M1117 is situated at the rear left of the vehicle's engine-cooling air-outlet louvers. This ASV belongs to the 4th Platoon, 527th MP Company Combat Support of the 709th MP Battalion, which is part of the 18th MP Brigade. Note the pattern of the Michelin 14.00 R20XZL tires and the towing eyes.

The ASVs of the 615th MP Company train mostly at the Grafenwöhr Training Area (GTA) located in south-east Germany. The M1117 Guardian is steered with hydraulic-power-assisted TRW Model TAS-65 steering. Like the M939 series 5-ton trucks, the ASV has a Central Tire Inflation System (CITS) that is controlled from the driver's station.

A close-up photo of the electrically driven Cadillac Gage Upgunned Weapon Station (UGWS). The UGWS features a Browning .50 caliber M48 Turret Mounted Machine Gun (TMMG) and a Rock Island Arsenal 40mm Mk.19 Mod 3 grenade launcher (which has been in use on the U.S. Marine AAVP7A1 for many years) situated in the middle of the hull. Note the Selectron M36E3 day/night sight and the strobe light.

surface selection is made. The ASV is different from other vehicles that use CTIS. The ASV has a completely independent high-pressure hydraulic brake system (up to 500 psi) that ensures quick stops. The resulting performance is impressive in a 13.4-ton vehicle. The first indication of a hydraulic leak is usually when the driver or team leader's seat stops working since they use the same hydraulic fluid as the brake system. Because of its 6.07-meter (20-foot) length and 2.56-meter (8.5-foot) width, the ASV can be either airlifted by C-130 (1 vehicle), C-141 (2 vehicles) and C-17 (6 vehicles) aircraft or by the CH-53 cargo helicopter. The ASV is not required to be air-dropable or sling-loaded under the CH-47 cargo helicopter.

The driver situated on the left has an excellent view through the armored glass windows to the front and the side of the ASV. The commander's station is situated on the right of the ASV in front of the turret. Both the driver's and commander's seats can slide up or down to allow a better view through the open hatches while driving the ASV. The two access hatches in the middle of the hull have firing ports that allow for firing personnel weapons under armor protection.

In the middle of the vehicle is the electrically driven Cadillac Gage Upgunned Weapon Station (UGWS) with a Browning .50 caliber M48 Turret Mounted Machine Gun (TMMG) and a Rock Island Arsenal 40mm Mk.19 Mod 3 grenade launcher, which the U.S. Marines have used in their AAVP7A1 for many years. There are 200 ready-to-fire12.7mm rounds and 96 40mm grenades stowed in the ASV turret. Also stowed in the hull of the M1117 are 600 12.7mm rounds and 576 40mm grenades. The two weapons of the UGWS, which have an elevation arc from +45° to -8°, are fed with ammunition from inside under complete armor protection. The Mk.19 Mod 3 grenade launcher has a rate of fire from 325-375 rounds per minute and an effective range of 2200 meters (2405 yards). The grenade's muzzle velocity is 240 m/s (787 f/s). The well-known .50 caliber TMMG has an effective range of 2000 meters (2186 yards) and a rate of fire of 550 rounds per minute. At the moment, the rotating UGWS, which is protected by a thin layer of ballistic steel armor and MEXAS armor, is not stabilized.

The gunner's seat is attached to a rail and can be slid up or down then locked into place by the small knob on the right of the seat. The spent shell container is located on the floor to the right of the seat and the control boxes for the gun laying system hang down from the turret in front of the gunner. Additionally, the crew is equipped with three 9mm M9 Berettas, two 5.56mm M4A1 Carbines and a M249 SAW.

The gunner uses the Selectron M36E3 day/night sight with 1x and 7x magnification situated in front of the turret hatch. He has a very good 360° view through the seven vision blocks that are arranged around the turret hatch. A fourth seat situated behind the UGWS is used as a spare seat. For night fighting capability, the driver and the commander may use AN/PVS-14 night vision goggles. For self-defense, in addition to the UGWS, the ASV incorporates a smoke and non-lethal turret-mounted grenade launching system consisting of eight M257 Light Vehicle Obscuration Smoke System (LVOSS) grenade launchers. The strobe light mounted on the M48 TMMG has a range of up to 1500 meters (1640 yards). Additionally, the ASV is equipped with an AN/PSN 11 Portable Lightweight GPS Receiver (PLGR) and an engine-fire extinguishing system. A hatch at the rear of the vehicle and a tunnel inside, which is also

This frontal view of the ASV M1117 Guardian shows the positions of the three crewmembers. If necessary, a fourth person can be transported by sitting on a spare seat behind the UGWS. Note the two roof hatches for the driver and the commander and the rear-view mirrors.

1:35 CENTAURO

Hubert Cance

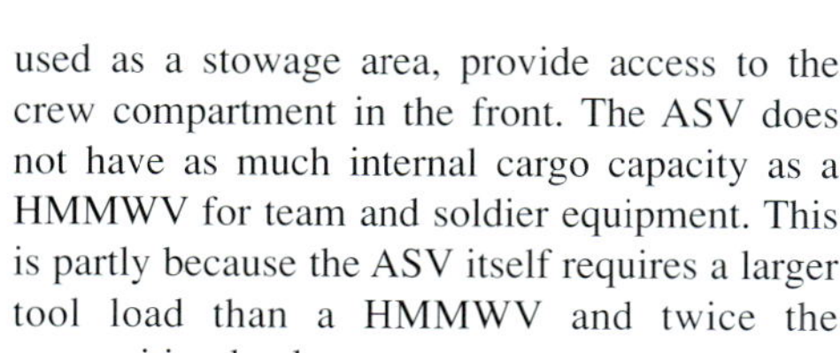

Side view of the M1117 Guardian. The modular expandable armor system (MEXAS), developed by the German Ingenieurbüro Deisenroth (IBD), consists of ceramic composite appliqué armor on the exterior surfaces and spall liner in the interior.

Access to the crew compartment is obtained through this door located at the rear of the vehicle. The MEXAS armor system is attached with screws to the main body of the ASV for easier replacement in case of damage.

For self-defense, the ASV also has a smoke and non-lethal turret-mounted grenade launching system consisting of eight M257 Light Vehicle Obscuration Smoke System (LVOSS) grenade launchers. Note the towing rope located behind the UGWS.

A view of the engine deck and the towing rope as seen from above. Note the engine air intake louvers, the mountings for the fuel cans, the SINCGARS antenna, and the orange safety light.

A close-up view of the Upgunned Weapon Station (UGWS), which is situated in the middle of the hull.

used as a stowage area, provide access to the crew compartment in the front. The ASV does not have as much internal cargo capacity as a HMMWV for team and soldier equipment. This is partly because the ASV itself requires a larger tool load than a HMMWV and twice the ammunition load.

A powerful recovery winch able to pull up to 6.8 tons by using a 50-meter (164-foot) long, 12.7-mm (.5-inch) thick steel cable situated at the front. Although the vehicle has a towing pintle in the rear, it can only be used to pull a tow bar. A standard trailer will impact the rear of the ASV during sharp turns due to the slope in the rear of the vehicle.

The ASV's communication system consists of two AN/VRC-91a radios and the AN/VIC-3 Vehicular Intercommunications System for crew communication. Along with the M42A2 NBC protection masks, the M13A1 NBC protection systems enable the ASV crew to operate in an NBC-contaminated environment. The vehicle is not over-pressurized but has a filtered, temperature-controlled, forced-air system that connects to the crew's M42A2 protective masks.

Unlike other Military Police troops, the ASV crews do not wear the regular battle dress uniform (BDU). Instead they wear olive Nomex fire protection overalls and the Combat Vehicle Crewman (CVC) helmet. This CVC helmet represents a convergence of technologies without compromise to offer high ballistic performance, durability, comfort, and improved communication. The Kevlar ballistic shell provides V50 ballistic test performance at a minimum of 427 mps (1,400 fps), while typical performance is 456 mps (1,500 fps). ASV crews use this helmet series with the M-138/G microphone and Mk-1697/G headset combined for a comfortable adjustable liner. A three-position switch allows radio, intercom and listen-in-only modes. Sound attenuation is maximized via ear cup design; outbound communications benefit from a microphone signal-to-noise ration of 15 dB. It has a fully adjustable liner and retention strap system. Padding materials provide comfortable protection from extreme temperature while significantly attenuating external noise. Sometimes the M1117 crews also wear the new

The UGWS viewed from the opposite side. The spent shell container is on the floor to the right of the seat. Note the attached spall liner in the interior and the floor plates.

Nomex BDUs used by helicopter crews. The introduction of a new stabilized Common Remote Operated Weapons System (CROWS), new night vision sights and a laser range finder is planned for the future.

MP Battalion Organization

Depending on the nature of the operation, corps Military Police units are usually among the first forces deployed to support military operations around the world. They deploy early to areas devastated by natural or man-made disasters to assist with disaster relief and damage assessment efforts. They provide security and force protection to friendly forces, critical facilities, and resources as units organize for military operations.

In a developing theatre, corps MPs concentrate mission support to the main effort. Units whose assistance to the main effort is vital normally receive the highest priority for protection. Key facilities, such as traffic choke

The Browning .50 caliber M48 Turret Mounted Machine Gun (TMMG) has an effective range of 2000 meters (2186 yards) and a rate of fire of 550 rounds per minute. At present the rotating UGWS, which is protected by a thin layer of ballistic steel armor and the MEXAS armor, is not stabilized.

This photo shows the rear access hatch in the open position. The tunnel in the background can also be used as a stowage area or for an emergency exit. Note the hydraulic cylinder, the handles of the hatch, and the mounting of the rear light.

The commander's station is located to the right of the driver. All crewmembers wear the Nomex Battle Dress Uniform (BDU) and Combat Vehicle Crewman (CVC) helmets. ASV crews use this helmet series with the M-138/G microphone and MK-1697/G headset unit for a comfortable adjustable liner. Both the driver's and commander's seats can be slid up or down to allow a better overview through the open hatches while driving the ASV.

The ASV M1117 Guardian crew consists of the driver, the gunner and the tank commander. The vehicle is not over-pressurized but has a filtered, temperature-controlled, forced-air system that connects to the crew's M42A2 protective masks.

points, critical tunnels and bridges, and ammunition and fuel storage points may require special protection. As the theatre matures, the focus may quickly change to other functions as the Military Police adjust priorities to accommodate the change.

A corps Military Police battalion is organized with a Headquarters and Headquarters Detachment (HHD) and three MP Companies Combat Support .

The Headquarters and Headquarters Detachment is divided into a battalion headquarters and detachment headquarters. All battalion activities are co-ordinated and controlled by the battalion headquarters, which consists of the specific sections and teams. The MP battalion is commanded by a Lieutenant Colonel, who forms the battalion command section together with the Executive Officer (XO) and the Battalion Command Sergeant Major. The operations section (S-3) and the intelligence section (S-2) form the Tactical Operations Center (TOC), which co-ordinates the activities of the three MP companies.

The TOC's vehicle park includes three HMMWVs and a M934 expansible van. Additionally, the battalion has an S-1 section with a HMMWV, which provides administrative and legal support and helps the MP battalion's commander to provide for the welfare of the battalion's personnel. The maintenance and repair of the innumerable battalion computer and communication systems is the area of responsibility of the communication section (S-6), which is equipped with two HMMWVs

Since the 212th MP Company from Kitzingen, Germany had not yet been equipped with the ASV M1117 Guardian, they used vehicles of the 615th MP Company from Vilseck, Germany during Mission Rehearsal Exercise "Mountain Guardian VIII".

This ASV M1117 Guardian secured Camp Albertshof during Mission Rehearsal Exercise "Mountain Guardian VIII" in the CMTC-Hohenfels, Germany. All ASVs are delivered with the standard NATO three-color camouflage pattern.

and a cargo trailer. The battalion supply is supervised by the S-4 officer. His section, which is equipped with a HMMWV and a M939 series 5-ton truck, co-ordinates the overall supply activities of the MP battalion. The battalion support section, which has four M939 series 5-ton trucks, a M105A2 cargo trailer and a M1061A1 cargo trailer, provides scheduled support to the HHD and the three MP companies. The mission of the unit ministry team, with its HMMWV, is to provide religious services and conduct soldier welfare ministries. The detachment headquarters, which provides command and control, administrative, supply, and co-ordinates security for the HHD, is equipped with two HMMWVs, two M939 series 5-ton trucks and three trailers .

Currently, the ASV-equipped corps MP companies are organized as follows. The company headquarters, which is equipped with two HMMWVs, four M939 5-ton trucks and three trailers, provides maintenance, supply, communications, and mess support to the unit. The MP Operations Center supports the unit's operation, conducting and planning with its four HMMWVs and a cargo trailer. The combat medic section provides company medical support with a HMMWV and a cargo trailer.

At present, additional funding for the ASV has been cancelled. However, the first 96 vehicles have already been paid for and will continue to roll off the production line until 2004 or 2005. Prior to that time, the U.S. Military Police School in Fort Leonard Wood, MO, will decide whether to request further funding for the remaining vehicles that are required.

M1117 Guardian

The Selectron M36E3 day/night sight with 1x and 7x magnification is situated on top of the Upgunned Weapon Station. Note the cover for the Rock Island Arsenal 40mm Mk.19 Mod 3 grenade launcher. Also of note is the anti-slip coat on the top the hull.

Most of the time, M1117 Guardians patrol along with M1025 High Mobility Multipurpose Wheeled Vehicles (HMMWV). Even though the ASVs have better armor protection and firepower, the HMMWVs provide better short-range vision and can check the roadway ahead for bridges and obstructions that might not support the 13.4-ton ASV.

The initial fielding plan is to disperse the 12 ASVs in each corps MP company among the four line platoons so that each one has three ASV's. These line platoons will be organized into a platoon headquarters with a HMMWV with cargo trailer and three squads with an ASV M1117 Guardian, two HMMWVs and one cargo trailer .

The MP squad leader would operate from one of the HMMWV teams. The HMMWVs provide better short-range vision and can check the roadway ahead for bridges and obstructions that might not support the ASV. The ASV offers surveillance from a longer range, and if the unit is attacked the ASV will provide the ability to stay to allow the HMMWV teams to maneuver away from danger.

Unlike most combat arms platoons that maneuver together in formation, the MP platoon most often operates independently and dispersed over a large area. The platoon conducts combat operations, when required, through the employment of mobile combat systems containing three-man teams operating independently or in concert. They are armed with crew-served and individual weapons capable of defeating a threat and defending a position against dismounted threats.

The MP platoon is capable of operating day or night, in various terrain conditions, and under all weather and visibility conditions. Their mode of operation is possible through the deployment and employment of the three-person team throughout the battlefield. However, it is dependent on its parent unit for sustained support. Because of extensive police training and law enforcement missions, MPs are highly skilled in the use of force and the employment of lethal and non-lethal technology, information collecting and dissemination, observation and surveillance, and crowd control. The MP platoon has a tremendous combat and non-combat information-collecting capability. This capability is the result of extensive area, zone, and route reconnaissance; daily contact with local nationals; conducting combined police patrols with host nation military and civilian police agencies; and conducting field interviews.

In November 2002, when the 212th MP Company deployed to Kosovo during KFOR 4B, they used the 12 ASVs that were already being used by Task Force Falcon. This photo shows to advantage the details of the upper hull of the M1117.

An MP platoon is capable of covering 500 square kilometers (311 square miles) in rolling terrain. However, more severe terrain such as mountains, METT-TC (Mission, Enemy, Terrain, Troops, Time available, and Civilian considerations) and mission objectives will affect this capability. For example, consider one mobile MP team per 10 kilometers (6 miles) of route coverage. For area coverage, begin with an estimate of one mobile MP team per 55 square kilometers (34 square miles).

After all of the initial fielding is completed in 2005, the platoon headquarters will receive three ASVs for a total of 15 M1117s in each corps MP company. We will probably see the Armored Security Vehicle M1117 Guardian very often during future missions outside the USA, such as in Kosovo, Afghanistan and Iraq. At the moment, the manufacturer, TM&LS, offers 18 versions based on the ASV, e.g., an Armored Personnel Carrier, a Command Post Carrier, an Ambulance Vehicle, and a Recovery Vehicle. Because of its capability for improvements, the ASV M1117 Guardian will be in use for a long time to come.

Acknowledgments

The author would like to thank MAJ Steve Green (18th MP Brigade), CSM Geraldine Rimpley (793rd MP BN), the 4th Platoon "Vipers", 615th MP Company in Vilseck, and CPT Mark Van Hout and MSG John Cavanaugh (HHC VIPERS CMTC) for their outstanding support.

Even though the ASV M1117 Guardian is only 6.07 meters (20 feet) long and has a crew of only three soldiers, it offers the U.S. Military Police companies excellent firepower and mobility, which is essential for current and future peacekeeping and peacemaking missions. Because of the many de-escalation scenarios practiced during the MRE "Mountain Guardian VIII" in 2002, the Armored Security Vehicles were very seldom used. When they were used, it was mostly as a Quick Reaction Force (QRF) to support the HMMWV-equipped MP squads.

The Upgunned Weapon Station (UGWS) of this ASV M1117 Guardian is not equipped with the .50 caliber barrel for the M2 machine gun and the 40mm barrel for the Mk.19 Mod 3 grenade launcher. Note the Combat Vehicle Kill Indicator (CVKI), which belongs to the MILES II laser engagement system mounted on the turret.

A Private First Class of the 630th MP Company from Bamberg, Germany observes the surroundings while his comrades arrest a war criminal in the CMTC MINI MOUT Kittensee. The 5.56mm M4A1 is a lightweight, gas-operated, air-cooled, magazine-fed, selective-rate, shoulder-fired weapon with a collapsible stock.

It is common for U.S. soldiers to wear privately owned sun glasses and other equipment, such as camel back hydration systems. Note the Specialist rank insignia on the PASGT body armor and the MILES II sensor equipment.

793rd Military Police Battalion Distinctive Unit Insignia "Facta Cum Honore" (Achievement with Honor)

The colors green and yellow are the colors of the Military Police Corps. The heraldic bend charged with red torteaux symbolizes the Battalion's route-security and circulation-control mission on the famous Red Ball Highway across France and Belgium and into Germany during World War II. The two torteaux represent campaign honors awarded for operations in World War II.

18th Military Police Brigade Patch

On a shield with a yellow border, a green shield bearing the yellow silhouette of Roman fasces charged with a green sword, point up.

Green and yellow are the colors of the Military Police Corps. The fasces, an ancient symbol of the magistrate's authority, and the sword for the military are combined to symbolize military law and order

Although U.S. Army Europe soldiers were issued black berets in February 2002, they still use the BDU cap in the field. This soldier carries a 5.56mm M4A1 Carbine and a 9mm M9 Beretta, which replaced the M1911A1 pistol.

Prior to the beginning of a patrol through the CMTC-Hohenfels using M1117s and HMMWVs, a platoon leader describes the mission to his two squad leaders during Mountain Guardian VIII. Note the patch of the 18th Military Police Brigade on his sleeve.

"Niedersachsenderby 2001"
1.*Panzerdivision* in River Assault

Walter Böhm

Most of the time, the first tank in a convoy is the company commander's vehicle. Here the company commander of 4.Kompanie PzLBtl 93 uses his signalling disk to indicate a change of direction to the tanks behind him. To avoid confusion during a road march, every tank commander must show the change of direction to the following vehicle. (Clemens Nießner)

The 1.(GE) *Panzerdivision* Crosses the Weser River

Between 11 and 16 November 2001, the German *Bundeswehr*'s 1.*Panzerdivision* held Exercise "Niedersachsenderby 2001" in the northern German lowlands. The exercise area was located between the cities of Bremen, Hannover and Diepholz. "Niedersachsenderby 2001" was a division-scale command-post exercise with the same fully equipped units and elements of a FTX (Field Training Exercise). There were 1800 soldiers, along with 450 wheeled and 180 tracked vehicles, and even some helicopters, deployed in the field.

Units Participating in the Exercise

The majority of the units were under order of the 1.(GE) *Panzerdivision*, based with its headquarters in Hannover, Lower Saxony. The 1.*Panzerdivision* is under order of the I.(GE/NL) Korps headquartered in Münster. The *Wehrbereichskommando* II/1.(GE) *Panzerdivision* in Hannover is composed of the following three active combat brigades: *Panzergrenadierbrigade* 1, *Panzergrenadierbrigade* 7 "Hansestadt Hamburg", and *PanzerLehrbrigade* 9. Since the last reorganization measures of the German *Bundeswehr*, with its motto "*Das neue Heer für neue Aufgaben*" ("The New Army for New Threats"), it is no longer possible to assign the units or brigades by their numbers or names to the commanding divisions. The same is true for the assignment of the companies or battalions to their commanding brigades. The 1.(GE) *Panzerdivision*'s assigned brigades took part in Exercise "Niedersachsenderby 2001" with their headquarters and the subordinate battalions' headquarters. Some fully equipped units participated in the FTX portion of the exercise.

Main Goal of the Exercise

"Niedersachsenderby 2001" was the largest exercise under control of the 1.*Panzerdivision* in 2001. The main focus of the maneuver was the training of the staff units and the training and exercising of NATO defense operations. During the entire exercise time, two brigade headquarters and six battalion headquarters were mobile in the exercise area. Another main point of the exercise was the deployment and march operations of combat vehicles and the river crossing over the Weser River at night and during the day. The river crossing operation was supported by the new M3 amphibious bridging and ferrying system. This bridging system is relatively new and the *Bundeswehr's* most modern engineer equipment.

Deployment of the M3 Amphibious Bridging System near the Town of Schinna

The high point of Exercise "Niedersachsenderby 2001" was undisputedly the daytime and nighttime river crossing operations over the Weser River near the town of Schinna. The materiel and vehicles from 15 fully equipped companies with *Schützenpanzer* Marder 1A3s, *Panzerhaubitze* M109A3GEA2s, *Kampfpanzer* Leopard 2A4s, and *Raketenwerfer* MARS rocket launcers had to be transported by road from the main assembly area near Nienburg to the crossing site near Schinna, and then further to the training area on the west bank of the Weser River.

At the crossing site, a war bridge was erected by means of the M3 amphibious bridging systems of *Schweres Pionierbataillon* (sPiBtl) 130, the heavy engineer battalion based in Minden. The bridge created by the M3 at the crossing site had an overall length of 106 meters (348 feet). The M3 bridge has a capacity for vehicles up to MLC 70 (Military Load Class). When vehicles drive at a speed of 25km/h (16 mph), 250 vehicles can cross the bridge in one hour. By comparison, the American-built Ribbon bridge system has a capacity of 100 vehicles crossing at a maximum speed of 10km/h (6 mph). This is one of the main advantages of the M3 and shows the high performance of the M3 fast floating bridge amphibious equipment. The M3 system was introduced to the German *Bundeswehr* units and the British Army units in 1996.

"Leopard Leaping across the Weser River". A fully camouflaged Leopard 2A4 MBT under order of 4./PzLBtl 93 crosses the M3 bridge near the town of Schinna. A small German flag is fastened to the antenna. Notice the Sachsenross (Saxon cross), the symbol of 1.Panzerdivision, on the flag. The main weapon of the Leopard 2A4 is the L44 120mm gun built by Rheinmetall. This smoothbore gun can destroy all known armor up to a distance of 2500 meters (2733 yards).

Scenario of the River Crossing

First, units of *Schweres Pionierbataillon* 130 scouted out the crossing site. Then the M3 units moved to their assembly areas 3 kilometers (1.8 miles) from the crossing site. The assembly areas of the combat troops were located closer to the river. Based on tactical orders, a river crossing was carried out only at night to protect the troops and to make identification and observation more difficult for the hostile reconnaissance troops. The company commanders and platoon leaders received a briefing at the crossing site from the engineers, then the M3 units erected the bridge. Finally, the combat elements were informed to begin their advancing operation. The different convoys had to pass checkpoints and were escorted by liason officers to the crossing site. At night, the vehicles drove under combat conditions with headlights switched off, and night vision equipment was used.

Air defense of the war bridge near Schinna against hostile aircraft was provided compliments of FlakPz Gepard. Following a series of simulated air strikes by helicopters and Tornado aircraft, the engineers had to replace damaged or destroyed (simulated) bridge parts with reserve M3 systems.

Summary

After the completion of "Niedersachsenderby 2001", the units redeployed to the Nienburg garrison. There the heavy elements were loaded onto railway freight cars and were redeployed to their home bases. The exercise ended on 16 November 2001 without any major accidents. For the participating units, the training in the field was more effective than the training at the well-known training areas. On the other hand, exercises like this are more expensive and require more logistic and administrative efforts.

The coordination and control of the main traffic and convoys was supported by *Feldjäger* units (German military police) and civilian police. When heavy equipment, such as battle tanks, is involved in an exercise, traffic coordination becomes vital. During the exercise, the autumn weather caused military vehicles to deposit a lot of mud and dirt on the civilian roads. Also, overwide vehicles had to be led through small streets,

Powered by the 1500hp engine, the Kpz Leopard 2A4 can reach a maximum speed of 70km/h (44 mph). The 55-ton heavy tank has a maximum range on roads of 400km (248 miles). (Michael Neumann)

"PanzerLehr Leopard 2A4". The 120mm main gun of the Leopard 2A4 MBT is supported by an integrated fire control system with a ballistic computer, fully stabilized sights, and a laser range finder. The "L" on front of the turret is the symbol of PanzerLehrbataillon 93. This unit belongs to PanzerLehrbrigade 9, which is based in Munster. (Michael Neumann)

Rear view of a Leopard 2A4 of PanzerLehrbataillon 93. The stenciled "400" on the right rear of the turret marks this tank as belonging to the company commander of 4.Kompanie, PzLBtl 93. (Michael Neumann)

and it was difficult to recognize well-camouflaged military vehicles in twilight and at night.

Another main issue was the coordination between the goals of the exercise and the rules regarding environmental conservation, especially when vehicles are driving across open land or are being refueled in the field. All of these things must be planned in agreement with civilian and military administration.

History of 1.(GE) *Panzerdivision*

The history of 1.*Panzerdivision* can be traced back to 1.*Grenadierdivision*, which was activated on 1 July 1956. The 1.*Grenadierdivision* was founded by the main elements of the former *Grenzschutzkommando Nord* (German border police). In 1959, the 1.*Grenadierdivision* was renamed 1.*Panzergrenadierdivision* and was active until 1 April 1981. The 1.*Panzergrenadierdivision* cooperates closely with the 1.(UK) Armoured Division (based in Verden from 1974-93), in the NATO defense concept. The German and the British units built

up a friendly partnership during the Cold War years. With the reorganization of the German *Bundeswehr* under the *Heeresstruktur 4* concept, the 1.*Panzergrenadierdivision* was renamed 1.*Panzerdivision* on 1 April 1981. With the end of the Cold War and the reunification of the Federal Republic of Germany and the German Democratic Republic, 1.*Panzerdivision* sent off a command and support group to control and carry out the dissolution of the NVA 1.*Motorisierte Schützendivision* based in Potsdam, and to build up new structures for the Bundeswehr. As a result, one main goal of the new Bundeswehr *Heeresstruktur 5* was realized: the merger of *Feldheer* and *Territorialheer* (*Bundeswehr* active and reserve units).

The 1.(GE) *Panzerdivision* is a large unit belonging to the *Hauptverteidigungskräften* (main defence forces); the division has 20,000 active soldiers. After mobilization in case of crisis or war, the unit can be reinforced with reserve units and achieve a strength of up to 57,000 soldiers. The division patch, a white Saxon horse on a red background positioned on a yellow and white shield, is a symbol for the friendship with and attachment to the country of Lower Saxony. Lower Saxony adopted the Saxon horse on its national flag in 1952.

Units Participating in the River Crossing during Exercise "Niedersachsenderby 2001"
4./ PzGrenBtl 332
6./ PzGrenBtl 332
4./ PzBtl 24
5./ PzBtl 24
4./ PzLBtl 93
4./ PzAufklLBtl 3
2./ PzArtBtl 15
4./ PzFlakRgt 11
4./ sPiBtl 130
1./ RakArtBtl 12
2./ RakArtBtl 12
StKp LogRgt 1
4./ InstBtl 11
2./ TrspBtl 11
2./ InstBtl 3

After the march from Nienburg to the river-crossing area, a Kpz Leopard 2A4 of 5./PzBtl 24 takes up a position in the assembly area. The tank is not camouflaged by netting against hostile aircraft. Notice the parts of the AGDUS training system on the turret. The stenciled "Potter" in white letters is the name of the tank commander. This identification practice is common on most tanks in a German PzBtl. In 2004, PzBtl 24 will be deactivated after 44 years of duty because the Heer has fewer tank units in the new structure of the Bundeswehr. (Michael Neumann)

"*Big Cats Take a Drink*". *The different fuel tanks of the Leopard 2A4 have an overall capacity of 1200 liters (317 gallons). During peace time, the Leopard 2A4 is gassed up with a maximum of 1000 liters (264 gallons) of diesel fuel.*

The Bergepanzer 3 *"Büffel" is based on an improved chassis of the well-known Leopard 2 MBT. The German* Bundeswehr *received their first* Büffel *in 1992. The* Büffel *replaced the* Bergepanzer 2A2 Standard *(based on the Leopard 1 chassis). In 1997, the* Bundeswehr *had a total of 75* Büffel *recovery tanks in their inventory.*

Order of Battle for 1.(GE) *Panzerdivision*

The 1.(GE) *Panzerdivision* is divided into three combat brigades: *Panzergrenadierbrigade* 1, *Panzergrenadierbrigade* 7 "Hansestadt Hamburg" and *Panzerlehrbrigade* 9.

Panzergrenadierbrigade 1:

Panzergrenadierbrigade 1 was activated on 1 April 1958 as *Kampfgruppe* B1(neu) in Hildesheim. *Kampfgruppe* B1(neu) was renamed *Panzergrenadierbrigade* 1 on 16 March 1959. The *Panzergrenadierbrigade*, which belongs to the *Hauptverteidigungskräften* (Typ B1), contains the following main units:

Panzergrenadierbataillon 12
Panzergrenadierbataillon 332
Panzerbataillon 24
Panzerartilleriebataillon 15
Panzerpionierkompanie 10

Panzergrenadierbrigade 7 "Hansestadt Hamburg"

Panzergrenadierbrigade 7 was founded on 1 August 1959 in Hamburg based on elements of the former 1.*Panzergrenadierdivision*. The brigade was first under order of 3.*Panzerdivision*. When 3.*Panzerdivision* was deactivated in 1996, the brigade came under order of 1.*Panzerdivision* in Hannover. *Panzergrenadierbrigade* 7 "Hansestadt Hamburg" belongs to the *Hauptverteidigungskräften* (Typ B1) and has following main units:

Panzergrenadierbataillon 72
Panzergrenadierbataillon 323
Panzerbataillon 74
Panzerartilleriebataillon 325
Panzerpionierkompanie 320

Panzerlehrbrigade 9:

Panzerlehrbrigade 9 was activated on 1 July 1956 in Münster under the name *Panzerkampflehrgruppe*. The brigade was renamed *Panzerlehrbrigade* 9 on 1 February 1959. The brigade was under order of 3.*Panzerdivision* until 1996. Today the *Panzerlehrbrigade* is under order of 1.*Panzerdivision* and belongs to the *Hauptverteidigungskräften*(Typ B1). It consists of the following main units:

Panzergrenadierlehrbataillon 92
Panzerlehrbataillon 93
Panzerlehrbataillon 334
Panzerartillerielehrbataillon 95
Panzerpionierlehrkompanie 90

In all, 15 companies rolled over the bridge created by the M3 bridging system near Schinna. Before the first vehicles could cross the bridge, a Bergepanzer 3 Büffel *had to test the capacity and security of the M3 bridge.*

Schützenpanzer *Marder 1A3s* of *4./PzGrenBtl 332* leave the railway station at Nienburg and head south to the river-crossing area. The Marder 1A3 vehicles were reloaded from freight cars. Since 1971, the Spz Marder has been the main combat vehicle for the Bundeswehr´s Panzergrenadieren. The vehicle was improved with some modifications. The last upgrading was the A3 improvement program. The main part of this modification was the improved armor protection of add-on armor plates. The vehicle´s weight increased by 5 tons by this measure. After 2008, the newly developed Spz "Panther" should replace the more than 30-year-old Spz Marder. (Michael Neumann)

"The Eyes and Ears of 1.Panzerdivision". The Luchs and Fuchs vehicles of PanzeraufklärungsLehrbataillon 3 support the 1.Panzerdivision units. In case of war or crisis, each of the three combat brigades under order of 1.Panzerdivision get one Panzeraufklärungskompanie of PzAufklLBtl.3. The PzAufklLBtl 3 is structured as follows: one Stabskompanie (Headquaters Company.), one Stabs/Versorgungskompanie (Headquaters/Support Company.), and three Panzeraufklärungskompanien (Armored Reconnaisance Companies.). (Michael Neumann)

The Spähpanzer *2A2 Luchs* reconnaissance vehicle has proven its reliability during deployment in the Balkans on various IFOR and SFOR missions and during KFOR operations. The Luchs is a quiet, fast, and highly mobile amphibious vehicle. In the A2 version, the Luchs is fitted with a thermal sight, a dual conveyor for the 20mm machine cannon, new bulletproof tires, and new radios with a wider range. (Eckhard Uhde)

A Panzeraufklärungskompanie (armored reconnaissance company) has 12 Spahpanzer *2A2 Luchs* vehicles and three Transportpanzer *Fuchs* fitted with the RASIT ground surveillance radar system. Only the PzAufklLBtl 3 is different. This battalion, which is still structured on the Heeresstruktur 5, has heavy reconnaissance platoons (schwere Spähtrupps) with Leopard 2A4 MBTs. (Michael Neumann)

The light armored reconnaisance platoons (leichte gepanzerte Spähtrupps), which are equipped with Luchs, receive support from the ground surveillance radar mounted on the Transportpanzer *1 Fuchs PARA RASIT*. The radar is named DR PT2a RASIT. The vehicle wears the tactical sign of 4.Kompanie PzAufklLBtl.3. Located on the right front underside of the vehicle is the battalion sign of PzAufklLBtl 3. (Eckhard Uhde)

A Transportpanzer *1 Fuchs RASIT* of *4./PzAufklLBtl 3* on its way to to the refueling point near the town of Hoysinghausen. The Fuchs RASIT system is an all-weather, night-and-day, ground surveillance radar system. The German Bundeswehr has a total of 1040 Fuchs vehicles in different versions in its inventory. The British Army and the US Army also use Fuchs vehicles. (Michael Neumann)

The FlakPz 1 Gepard has an effective firing range of up to 2500 meters (2733 yards) against aircraft and helicopters. Lightly armored vehicles and targets on the ground can be destroyed up to a distance of 1500 meters (1640 yards). The 35mm guns can be ready to fire just six seconds after the radar or the crew has tracked the target. The fire ratio is 550 rounds per minute with each machine cannon. The vehicle's hull is based on the Leopard 1 MBT chassis.

This Flugabwehrkanonenpanzer (self-propelled anti-aircraft gun) Gepard of 4.Batterie PzFlakReg 11 was deployed near the town of Schinna. These weapons would provide protection against aircraft when the units came in for the river-crossing operation. The FlakPz 1 Gepard, which is armed with two 35mm machine cannons, is a highly mobile, fully independent weapon system.

An upgraded Panzerhaubitze M109A3GEA2 of Panzerartilleriebataillon 15 on the march near Nienburg. This unit is under order of Panzergrenadierbrigade 1. There was a plan to replace all Panzerhaubitze M109A3GEs with the new Panzerhaubitze 2000 until the middle of the '90s. But due to the end of the Cold War and the reduced budget for national defense, only 185 Panzerhaubitze 2000s were delivered to the Bundeswehr. A life-increasing program for the old, but still operational, Panzerhaubitzen M109A3GE was required. The manufacturer, KUKA, developed a modification kit to update the aged vehicles to the M109A3GEA2 level. (Michael Neumann)

In the past, the Bundeswehr had more than 4000 M113s and variants in its tank fleet. Today, there are still 3000 M113s in different versions on duty. This M113A1 GfltPzArt (Rohr), which belongs to 2./PzArtBtl 15, is fitted with digitalized computers, printers, data links, and radios. The Funkleitpanzer Artillerie (FltPzArt) receives the data about targets from the forward observer's vehicle (BeobPzArt-Rohr). After this data is selected and controlled, the firing orders are given by radio to the howitzers. (Eckhard Uhde)

An upgraded PzH M109A3GEA2 of PzArtBtl 15 in firing position near the river-crossing site. The barrel of the gun, which is built by Rheinmetall and is the NATO-standard 155mm caliber, is 6874mm (22.5 feet) long. The gun barrel is very similar to the barrel of the towed FH 70. From the outside, the upgraded M109A3GEA2 can be identified by the additional stowage baskets on the front of the turret and the additional boxes on the rear of the turret and the rear of the hull. (Clemens Nießner)

PzH M109A3GEA2s from 2./PzArtBtl 15 advance to the crossing site near Schinna. The main goal of the M109A3GEA2 improvement program was to upgrade the projectile magazine, which now holds 24 ready-to-fire projectiles with fuses, and to modify the ammunition supply. Ten additional projectiles are stowed in newly designed racks right and left of the rear turret doors. Also, the charge magazine was modified for 34 charges. An electrically operated lift handle now makes it easier to stow projectiles. (Clemens Nießner)

The German version of the US Army's MLRS (Multiple Launch Rocket System) is known as MARS by the Bundeswehr (Mittleres Artillerie Raketen System). Raketenartilleriebataillon 12 supports 1.Panzerdivision with this highly effective weapon system. The main differences between the German-built MARS and the US-built MLRS are the improved tracks and rubber side skirts on the German vehicles. The rockets are identical and have a 227-mm (9-inch) diameter. There are 12 rockets in two pods, and both the MLRS and MARS have a fire ratio of 12 rockets in 50 seconds. (Clemens Nießner)

1.Panzerdivision

Bergepanzer 2A2 Standard recovery tank of RakArtBtl 12. The Bergepanzer 2A2 Standard recovery tank is the standard recovery vehicle for the Bundeswehr's Panzerbataillone equipped with Leopard 1 MBTs, the Panzergrenadierbataillone with Marder 1A3s, Panzerartilleriebataillon, Raketenartillertiebataillone MARS, and some seperate maintenance units. (Clemens Nießner)

The chassis of the BPz 2A2 Standard is based on the hull of the Leopard 1 MBT-vehicles family. The vehicle has a weight of 40.6 tons when ready for duty and fully equipped. The vehicle is fitted with a 270-degree turnable, hydraulically operated crane with a maximum lifting capacity of up to 20 tons. The vehicle has a blade for stabilizing the vehicle during crane operations and a 35-ton main winch. (Clemens Nießner)

These two Elefant SLT 50-3 tank transporters belong to 2.Kompanie of Transportbataillon 11. The Elefant tank transporter is designed to transport heavy loads on roads and across countryside. The difference between the SLT 50-2 and SLT 50-3 versions is a different powerpack. Note the elephant sticker on the front bumper. (Eckhard Uhde)

For the Bundeswehr's armored units, the heavy Elefant SLT 50-3 tank transporter has become a useful and necessary tool. Here an Elefant tractor tows a six-axle flatbed trailer. This heavy-load trailer, which is produced by Kässbohrer, has no cross-country capability. (Eckhard Uhde)

Ambulances are on alert during the whole exercise to give first aid to troops in case of an emergency. This ambulance truck belongs to StKpLogRgt 1. The ambulance is based on the Unimog 1300L chassis built by Daimler Benz. Its Bundeswehr code is Lkw 2t gl Krankenkraftwagen.

A M3 amphibious bridging vehicle of 4./sPiBtl 130 on the march to the river-crossing zone. The M3s are used to help combat troops cross medium and large rivers when the Biber bridgelayer is too short to span the gap. To increase maneuverability on the ground or on water, a hydraulic axle-control system provides rapid extention and retraction of the M3 axles. With this, the vehicle's overall height on the ground is decreased and the amount of water resistance and the depth of water necessary for floating are reduced. Its fuel consumption is 55 liters/100km (14.5 gallons/62 miles) of diesel fuel on the march and 65 liters (17 gallons)/hour when operating on water. Its fuel tanks have a capacity of 400 liters (106 gallons).

M3 amphibious bridging vehicles have all-wheel drive and possible all-wheel steering. The big low-pressure tires are fitted with a tire-pressure control system. When all-wheel steering is activated, the huge M3 has excellent mobility when driving through small towns or over rough terrain.

War bridge near Schinna. After all the required M3 units had entered the river, they were connected to a nearby bridge, then the engineer liason officer called for the first convoys to cross the Weser. Only 30 minutes elapsed from the time the first M3 units entered into the water to when the first Spähpanzer 2A2 Luchs reconnaisance vehicle of 4./PzAufklLBtl 3 crossed the river.

After the Panzeraufklärer had crossed the M3 bridge, the liason officers at the checkpoint called up the next convoy. Here a fully camouflaged Kpz Leopard 2A4 of 4./PzBtl 93 crosses the Weser River. Under wartime conditions, a river-crossing operation is carried out only during the nighttime whenever it is possible. This gives all the participating units better protection against hostile countermeasures.

The M3's engine compartment is located at the rear of the vehicle. The 347-hp BF 8 L 513 LC engine is built by KHD(Deutz). After the introduction of the M3 to the German and British heavy engineer units, Taiwan also ordered the M3 amphibious bridging system.

The hydraulically operated foldable side pontoons of this M3 are folded down in the water driving position. Having entered the Weser River, the M3 swims to the crossing site near the town of Schinna.

During water operations, the M3 is directed from a seperate pilot stand. With the left levers on, the vehicle can be steered in case of emergency, example, when electrical or hydraulic systems fail. The foldable pilot stand for water operations is mounted on the rear of the vehicle. Before driving into the water, it is folded upward and the vehicle is directed from this location.

ON FOCUS: Fast Floating Bridge Amphibious Equipment M3

The M3 amphibious bridging system is a highly mobile floating bridge and ferry equipment. The M3 drives independently on roads to the crossing site and can build immediately, without preparation, bridges or ferries for wheeled and tracked vehicles, with a capacity up to the military load class of MLC 70.

The Introduction and Deployment of the M3 by the German *Bundeswehr* and British Army

In 1996, the SSB (*Schwimm Schnell Brücke*) M3 was delivered to the *Bundeswehr* sPiBtl 130 (*Schweres Pionierbataillon*) based in Minden and to the British 28th Engineer Regiment based in Hameln, Germany. The SSB M3 replaced the older M2 amphibious bridge equipment system used by the *Bundeswehr* and the British Army. The sPiBtl 130 has 30 M3 systems in its two SchBrKp (*Schwere Brücken Kompanien*), each with 15 M3 vehicles. The British 28th Engineer Regiment is equipped with a total of 38 SSB M3s. The SSB M3 vehicles were built by the German manufacturer Fa.EWK, *Eisenwerke Kaiserslautern*.

A High-Performance Bridging System

Today, the SSB M3 is the most modern amphibious bridging and ferrying system in the world. Using the M3 system, military units can build bridges or ferries with a minimum of personnel and time, at prepared or unprepared crossing sites. Twenty-four soldiers can build a 100-meter-long bridge in 20 minutes. By comparison, it took 48 soldiers 45 minutes to build the same bridge using the M2 system, the M3's predecessor.

M3 in Action

The M3 vehicles can drive independently from the assembly area to the crossing site. Near the river the side pontoons are folded down and the vehicle can drive non-stop directly into the water. After the vehicles swim into position side by side, the roadway/ramp elements are positioned by the vehicle's own light crane. Then the vehicles are connected to ferries or a nearby bridge. Although the M3 is fitted with the most modern subsystems, this part of the operation requires a lot of concentration and skill on the part of the crew. During the building phase, the bridge is held in position by its hydrodynamic water jet propulsion system and the contact of the ramp elements on the banks. Additional fastening to the river banks by anchors is not necessary.

Technical Data

Length: 12.82m (42 feet)
Width with pontoons folded, traveling position: 3.35m (11 feet)
Width with pontoons unfolded, water position: 6.57m (22 feet)
Weight: 25.3 tons
Crew: 3
Engine output: 347 PS/252 kW
Speed on roads: 80 km/h (50 mph)
Speed in water: 14 km/h (9 mph)
Range (Road march): 725 km (450 miles)
Elapsed time for ferrying operation: 6.25 hours
Tire-pressure control system, switchable four-wheel steering, and differential lock on rear and front axle.